Combat Zone

The Value Based Proposition

The Open Framework Agreement:
The Guerrilla Warfare Sales Tactic!

The 4th book in the series

By

Dennis T Lewis

IMPORTANT NOTICE

The information, materials, concepts, digital media and intellectual property contained within this document are the sole property of CONTRAQ SOLUTIONS and are deemed proprietary and confidential. Any disclosure, copies or duplication of such materials or part thereof, in any form whatsoever may not be distributed without the explicit permission of CONTRAQ SOLUTIONS

management and training consultants

Postnet Suite 62
Private Bag X43
Sunninghill
2157
South Africa

Telephone	(011) 807 8699
Facsimile	(011) 807 8699
Cell Number	083 625 2613
e-mail	contraq@icon.co.za

www.contraqsolutions.com

Other books in the Combat Zone Series

Selling in the 21st Century

Negotiating in the 21st Century

Do Nothing Negotiation

Preface

Back in 1999 I wrote my first book: Combat Zone - 'Selling in the 21st Century'. I never thought I had it in me to write a book, so it was just as big a surprise to me as it was to all my closest friends, to have this book published and achieve some success!

Ever since, I have tried to continue this series of works with the books 'Negotiating in the 21st Century' and 'Do Nothing Negotiation, in an attempt to support the sales fraternity and all of the intrepid negotiators out there with tips on how to succeed in the world of selling and negotiation in the fast becoming global competitive village.

In this work **'The Value Based Proposition',** I have focused on giving the reader an insight into some of the successful strategies that I have worked on, with my clients over the last 2 years in the difficult task of breaking into competitive held strongholds and outmanoeuvring their competition; the customers supply chain processes and the bidding process to gain access into the customer's business! **Sound interesting?** Well, when I was tasked with the challenge by one of my customers back in 2012, it was!

How do you gain entry to a multinational company and its potential business when you have never done work with them; have no track record and have not even prequalified your company to receive any enquiries from them? In short, you're not even on their radar!

You use guerrilla warfare sales tactics that's how!

Interested now? Well read on and I'll share some secrets with you regarding the bidding system, financial motivational criteria, out gunning your competition and creating **account pursuit strategies, customer relationship management plans, negotiation strategies and open framework agreements** that can open up unimaginable opportunities for you and your company.

It's nothing new. It's all about creating **value based propositions** that your potential customer cannot afford to ignore!

It's about creating a situation where the decision for the customer is not: shall I do business with this company? But rather, **how will we justify our decision if we don't!**

This may be the thinnest book you buy this year, but it may be one of the most valuable investments you make. If you are in the selling game you need to read this book

Contents

6. **The Basic Framework Plan**
   - How to build a basic Framework agreement plan.
   - The elements of the plan in detail.

7. **The Executive Overview**
   - How to construct a framework offer covering letter or executive overview

8. **Protecting your Intellectual Property**
   - Why a non disclosure agreement
   - The tactic of the NDCA.

9. **The Strategic Positioning Statement**
   - Why a strategic positioning statement.
   - What should you include for?

10. **Scope Definition**
    - What are you offering your customer?
    - Defining roles, reporting structures and responsibility areas.
    - How to sell up and sell forward.

11. **Product and Service Definition**
    - The what, the why and the how.
    - How to leverage your position.

12. **The Strategic Account Management Team**
    - The team structure, the players and their roles.
    - The organogram.

13. **Performance Criteria**
    - Your teams working methodologies.
    - Deadlines and responsibilities.

14. **The Customer Relationship Management Plan**
    - What is a CRM plan?
    - The basic elements.
    - How to build one.

15. **The implementation Plan**
    - How are you going to roll out your framework plan?
    - The benefits of a phased approach.

16. **The Strategic Offer**
    - How to structure your strategic offer.

1.

Acknowledgements

Who to thank? That's a very difficult question because so many people have had an influence over what I do and what I write!

First and foremost I want to thank my dear old friend Brenda Aubert. We lost Brenda last year, 2014, to the big C. It was a terrible shock to anyone who knew her. Brenda was a contract buyer, a very good one, and in fact it was Brenda who came up with the title for my books "Combat Zone'. I knew Brenda for thirty years. She was a constant broad sword to my foil when discussing selling and buying strategies. The world will be a sadder place without her!

I would like to thank the team at Aucor, Jacques van de Linde, Charles Neser and Darren Winterstein! Without their involvement this book would never have been written.

My other customers: Steve Venter from Rittal, Steve Labram from Thermo Scientific. My very dearest friend Paul van Wyk from EagleBurgmann who has constantly challenged me to facilitate meaningful change in my customer's lives and that of my own!

The Discovery Heath team Sharon Forman, Louise Steyl and Linda Opie who helped me reinvent the Value

Based Proposition. Peter Skerritt who helped me reintroduces the concept to the banking fraternity! Go figure!

To Brian Howarth head of the Magnet Group, one of the most professional organisations I have had the pleasure to do business with, Reitte Fern from the Marsh organisation who has trusted me to train their sales and renewal teams in the art of the Value Based Proposition, and of course, the Honeywell Corporation where I learnt what it really meant to sell a value based proposition in the first place!

Last, but certainly not least, my beautiful wife Heather, who has constantly supported and motivated me over the good and bad times in the last 13 years and who helps to hone my negotiation skills on a daily basis!

To Brenda. You started this journey with me.

I miss you!

2.

Introduction

What is a **'Value Based Proposition?'** Do you have one? Has your organisation calibrated its success based on solutions guaranteed to provide your customers with additional value above and beyond the obvious benefits that your products or service offering provides? **More importantly can you prove that to the customer?**

Are you satisfied that the solutions that you offer to your customers are immediately attractive to them because of the value add they provide or, are you just throwing your hat into the ring along with your competitors and hoping for the best every time you submit a proposal?

In my experience, most of the time, the latter seems to be the case. "We add value to our customers' businesses" is one of the most over- used phrases in the selling game! Almost all of my clients, at one time or another, have told me that their market differentiator is that they add value to their customers' businesses. They may well do, However, when I ask them to show me a case study of how they have provided the customer with this value add: the what, how much, how and when they provided it, they can't! **It's never been documented!**

The problem is if they are not documenting these successes, even if they are providing an additional return on the investment for the customer, unless they are tracking it and actively documenting these results together with their customer, providing this value based proposition is like wetting yourself in a black business suit: **you get a nice warm feeling but nobody notices!**

This lack of calibrated success and the lack of demonstrable case studies are also carried over into the sales team's tool kit that they use to sell.

In almost all product and service presentations that I see, very little reference is made to the Value Based Proposition or any value adds at all! The presentations are simply based on the technical benefits of the product or service offering. They're as boring as hell and have very little compelling business content to differentiate them from any other competitor's offering!

Now this is a very big problem! How is the customer going to motivate a change to your product if you don't provide them with one?

In any sophisticated business with corporate governance, the customer has to submit a written motivation with a rock solid financial business model to buy anything today! It's part of the supply chain process! If you don't provide them with this information, how are they going to do this?

In reality they simply don't! It's too much trouble! Unless your product is a life-changing technology, the supply chain will simply add you to the bidders list with all the other competitors and you will have to take your chances when they issue the next tender!

This is a huge wasted opportunity because it's not as though the sales people don't know their products have these differentiators, but they skim over them because they are not documented.

Let me give you an example!

When I ask the sales engineers presenting to me: why any specific feature of their product is so important, only then do they inform me that either this or that feature can save a lot of money if used correctly!

Firstly, why that isn't stated clearly in the presentation is beyond me and secondly, when I ask them how much money can it save me, they don't know! What's happening here? What's happened to the good old **value based proposition?**

Is it me or has it just gone out of fashion to sell **compelling commercial arguments** designed to motivate the customer to buy?

The simple truth is that no self- respecting sales person is going to stick out their neck to quote any value based propositions when they don't know for sure what they are, and more importantly they have no benchmarking documentation to prove them!

The first initiative we can adopt from this work is to ensure that all of our sales presentations encompass the value based propositions our products and service offerings provide for our customers!

We have to back up these claims with documented benchmarking and case studies to prove to the customer we can do what we say we can!

If we want our customers to motivate the use of our products and services, the least we should be doing is providing them with the information to do just that!

A short while ago, one of my clients asked me to take a look at one of their product presentations they had just released to their sales teams internationally. When I enquired what the objective was, I was told that this particular presentation had been designed and compiled professionally and had cost thousands of dollars to produce, however, the sales people were complaining that the presentation was not having the desired effect on their customers and subsequently the product sales figures were well below planed expectation. Can I tell them what they were doing wrong?

After taking one look I was pretty sure I could identify some of the problems areas, let me list them for you.

- The presentation contained 67 slides.
- Most of the slides had no progressive exposure (no bullet or image animation.)
- Many slides contained more than 10 bullets of pure written information (de facto word document.)
- Some slides encompassed animated graphics (multiple slide effects from one mouse click.)
- Many references to unique product functionality without any explanation of why the functionality was desirable or even relevant to the application.

- Many slides depicted complicated circuitry diagrams and technical Data (again without any reference to why they were important.)
- **Absolutely no reference to any commercial justification or value based proposition at all!**

I'm sure that some of you professional presenters out there know why these simple problems can reduce a great presentation into a very bad one. (I'm going to cover all these elements of an intelligent presentation later in the book in more detail) but for now let's concentrate on the missing value based proposition.

This presentation was designed by an in house product specialist and an outside graphics design team. In short, it was designed by an engineer and the design team followed his instructions!
The presentation was designed to illustrate how clever and innovative the technical capabilities of this product could bring to a customer's application. If you simply wanted to impress another engineer on the technical aspects of this product at a purely intellectual level, this presentation was brilliant!
But that is not what it was designed to do!
It sole purpose was to sell the product!!!

If I could simply get this one message across to all you sales engineers out there that the products you are attempting to sell may be the most technically advanced gizmos in the universe, but unless you start building presentations that encompass the commercial benefits they can provide your customers you won't sell many of them!

You need to balance the presentation by demonstrating the product capabilities with the value based propositions they deliver due to these innovations!

In the case of my client's presentation, by discussing these innovative design capabilities with the product specialists and undertaking some research into the specific industrial application this product was designed for, we were able to define 12 value based propositions on a presentation that encompassed 16 slides!

By adding one animated bullet, per slide, indicating what each technological innovation would save the customers organisation in one year, in real Dollars, we came up with an astonishing 12 Thousand Dollar value based proposition per installation! For a product that cost 4 Thousand Dollars, that's a no brainer! The result we were able to increase the product sales by 22% in the next quarter!

We, it seems are relying too heavily on our engineers capabilities to demonstrate our product and service differentiators and forgetting we need to sell them based the commercial benefits they can provide our customers!

As we discuss more initiatives in this book it will become clear that the value based proposition is at the heart of each and every one of these initiatives and without this fundamental element none of them will work!

Ok, let's move on!

Here's another common symptom to add to the problems that selling organisations are experiencing:

During my research in 2013, I was surprised to find that in many organisations that I was consulting to, their 'Hit Rate', that is their overall percentage of successful proposals, was as low as 12%! That means that 88% of all their bids were unsuccessful! **88%!!!**

Given the above scenario we have discussed so far regarding the lack of value based propositions in our sales strategies you could be forgiven for believing this is the sole contributing factor for these sales metrics, but that's not the case!!

When discussing these metrics with sales managment I was often told "Oh that's normal for our business. In fact that's quite good!" Well in my day, in the Honeywell family, those kinds of sales metrics would have gotten you fired in a New York minute (that's 7 seconds!)

If you can only count on a 12% hit rate, what does your sales team's pipeline need to look like to ensure that you achieve your sales plan? Let me spell that out for you: If your divisional sales target is $20 Million, then your sales team's total combined pipeline will have to be $166 Million. That's crazy money! Where are you going to find that kind of business potential? Those ratios don't make sense!

Let me define some of the results from my research for you:

Hit rates are down to 12%

Market prediction is 65 – 70% of Target

That's a Failure rate of 88%

Sales Teams Are Customer Facing for less than 30% of their Time!

Pipe line must be 3X Target

Sales visits are Down to 2 per Day

Sales visits must increase by a factor of 3

It's Simple Math. To Succeed our sales teams need to do 3 X the work!

If we accept these metrics, then the sales management is going to have to play the **numbers game!** That means: driving the sale team into the ground by wanting them to visit 3 times the amount of customers to achieve the ratios they need to make target!

It gets worse!

Just the cost of running a sales team today, based on these kinds of returns, makes no sense. Based on the market you are in and the potential value of each order that you receive, how many basic sales calls are your sales team going to have to make to even come close to securing that kind of pipeline? Given these sales metrics, **you're not in the selling game, you're in a lottery!**

You would be forgiven for thinking that these sales teams are giving written proposals to their Taxi drivers and their brother in-law's! They're not of course. They are just trying to maximise their ability to sell by using the numbers game, but that's counterproductive! Why quote to a customer if you haven't got a cat's chance in hell of winning it!

It's not a quoting game; it's an orders game!

For every proposal that you lose, your organisation is going backwards and that's damaging your reputation. "Oh! You are the guys who lose more than you win!"

In addition, why quote to a customer if it's just become an administrative chore? If you don't have the time to actively sell it to the customer, don't bother, **your competitor will!**

My old boss used to say if an enquiry lands on your desk and you knew nothing about it prior to that, throw it in the bin! It's been decided already! If you weren't called in by the customer to discuss your offering someone else has, and this enquiry is a pricing exercise:

You have more chance of falling pregnant than of winning it!

Again, if your sales team is using an 'also ran' technique, asking customers if they can just have a chance to quote against their main supplier, you are also fooling yourselves. These just prop up an already exaggerated pipeline of potential business that you won't win!

If you're suffering from any of these symptoms don't feel bad, you're in very good company!

You have to free up your sales team to do what they are paid for and that is: to **SELL!** Not babysit your captive customers. They have to really sell to compete. They have to increase their face time with customers and put real effort into selling the value based propositions that you have. **But you have to have one in the first place!** Where are your case studies and your benchmarking data? If you don't have any, your salespeople are selling using outmoded techniques!

In my research it now appears that sales people are spending less than 30% of their time customer facing! In an average 40 hour week that's 12 hours! If you factor in the travel and waiting time, that comes out to about 6 customer visits per week! Given the sales metrics that we have just discussed, that simply won't cut it! I don't want to sound like an old geezer but in my day, salespeople were expected to see 5 customers a day! What's happened?

I have always said that salespeople are like Ferraris, you should drive them, pedal to the metal, but you have to fill them up with gas and drive them before they can go anywhere! But have you ever seen a Ferrari pulling a trailer?

These are the sales metrics we should be aiming at:

70% customer facing is on average 3 days a week visiting customers. The best use of our sales teams can be made by getting them to give group presentations to 20 or 30 customers at a time. This can result in a single sales person having face time with over 30 customer's per week!

The use of probability score cards. (Deciding when to quote and when not to, based on the probability of success) can save your sales team hours of wasted time. Unfortunately the above scenario is rare!

Today, it seems that, more times than not, the salespeople are stuck in their office doing administrative work and preparing proposals! That's not what you should pay them for! Their job is to **SELL!**

When I ask sales teams to define an average week in their lives, I am normally confronted with the fact that about 70% to 80% of their time is spent taking care of the existing customers that they have chasing administrative stuff!

Almost no time is spent in capturing new business! We need to manage our captive customers, not have them manage us! Far too much time is spent managing these customers with very little business revenue being generated.

In fact, in many organisations that I deal with, their strategic customers have become major resource and profit sapping liabilities, not assets! This is due to the unprecedented service levels that the customer is demanding, but not paying for, and the constant pressure from the customer to reduce pricing to retain their business!

This happens in a buyer's market. The main contributing factor in this scenario seems to be the inability of the sales organisation to sell their value added services instead of just product! The customers are managing them not the sales organisation managing the customer. How do they manage us? Let me show you:

This is common; in many organisations, because the sales team do not have a customer relational management plan (CRM) they find themselves run ragged keeping up with the demands from their customers. This is partly due to working in a buyer's market; however, if you fail to plan you're planning to fail! We have to manage our current customer base more efficiently.

Take after sales service as another example of how we battle to sell our service offerings to our captive customers.

Many organisations really battle to sell their after sales service offering. This is seen as a different cost centre to the sales department. A cost centre! Not a profit centre? This is a self-defeating mind set. If you just sell product without the after sales service package then you are selling a commodity and in the commodity business, **the only differentiator is price!**

More time needs to be spent on selling the value based proposition of the organisations total capabilities to their customer's! Most organisations have two sets of salespeople selling service as a separate entity. It's an afterthought.

This, I believe, is a huge wasted opportunity! In my experience, once the customer has been persuaded to do the math, to provide the after service element of any product that they buy themselves, costs them twice as much as letting the supplier do it for them!

The contributing factors are many, but the real problem is, in most cases, that the customers do not appreciate this fact as this value add is not sold aggressively enough by the product sales teams in the initial product sale!

Sales organisations still rely too much on the individual capabilities of their salespeople! Today, we need to realise that: to sell successfully, we need to sell in focused teams, selling the total organisational capabilities as a package deal!

What can you do to change this? Well, you need Account Managers! People who 'farm' the strategic customers while your sales team finds new ones!

Here's one way to free up your sales team to sell!

The solution is to embark on an aggressive Customer Relationship Management regime (CRM) with your strategic customers!

In today's market, the returns generated by doing business the same way with every customer that you have and using your sales team to manage them, simply makes no sense! This is why the sales team is customer facing for only 30% of their time! Instead of looking for more business, the salesperson is now stuck with their captive customer base and, to be frank, they are not the right animal to manage them! Their organisation has turned them into an account manager/salesperson! (I will be going into the CRM process in more detail in chapter 4)

This situation is more dangerous than you think! We want our sales people to find new business and look after the business that we already have, but we only pay them to look after the existing business!

What do I mean? Well think about it: salespeople are generally paid commission on the business that they bring into the organisation, right? They have to make ends meet and plan their lives around the salaries and commission that they make. If you were them, what would put this monthly commission at risk? How about chasing new business, which may take three months to secure and represents high risk? **Or should they simply farm the customers they already have on a monthly basis and pray these customers will spend 20% more with them this year! Because that's what has worked for them in the past?**

We aren't paying them to grow the business; we are paying them to maintain the status quo!

This is the most common symptom that I come across in the un-calibrated sales organisation. The remuneration system! Almost all the organisations that I come across pay their salespeople some form of commission, but they structure it incorrectly. If you want a sales team to focus on securing new business then you have to pay them accordingly!

By now I'm sure that you can appreciate that all the symptoms that we have discussed above are systematic of a **non-calibrated sales organisation**. It seems that these organisations are working very hard but actually don't know what really works and what guarantees success!

We may need to re-examine our sales team structure; redefine roles and the selling strategy and pay our sales teams correctly!

You have to pick your battles and the battlefield to overcome your competitors so, CRM or the strategic account management of selected customers by a small effective team can provide you with the kind of return on investment that makes sense.

As I stated above, once you have calibrated the organisation's solutions to fit the needs of one strategic customer, you can then use this model and experience to capture further strategic business!

However, when it comes to plain product, you have a decision to make: what business are you in? Apart from the product warrantee, you should be selling these commodities without any frills at all! "How many do you want and what colour would you like?" "Oh! You would like an instruction manual with that would you? Ok that will be $20 extra!"

That's why, sometimes, the price of your competitor's products are so cheap! Cheap is the right word: cheap and cheerful! No value add and no frills!

If you want to be in the commodity business then you have to gear your organisation to be in one and not straddle both market segments using the same selling techniques!

You can be in both, but you have to restructure your sales team! They need to be able to distinguish between the simple product sell and the tactical or strategic opportunity, and then you need the right people to handle both!

This is where CRM and the framework strategic offer can be your most valuable tool to gain entry to your competitor's strongholds. In short, you have a calibrated, 'Value Based Proposition' that you can prove works! In both product and strategic opportunities, this can change the odds in your favour in a big way!

However, we are missing a step! Even If we are able to free up our sales teams to sell, we still have to find this new customer and how do we gain entry into their business?

Before we can entice them into a CRM Programme or framework agreement offer, we have to secure their interest first! Let's explore a sure-fire way to break into a new customer using a **specific market segment benchmarking survey approach; it's the second of the six initiatives we will explore in this book!**

3.

The Benchmarking Survey Approach

How many of us have been asked to participate in a survey questionnaire? And, what's more to the point, how many of us have had access to the results of that survey once it has been completed? Not many, I'll wager! Well, think about focusing on a specific market segment in your business: let's say, for argument's sake, the pharmaceutical business, and running a benchmarking survey to determine what is happening in that market segment focusing on your specific business offering!

Do you think the customers would want to participate if you promised them that you would present your findings to them after you have completed the survey? Well, what do you think? Let's find out by reviewing a recent customer survey conducted in the fortune 500 arena in 2014!

Customers were asked what they want from sales teams on their first approach in pursuit of business with them. Here are their answers:

What Customers Want

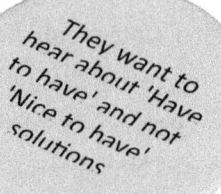

You need to present the solutions that guarantee results based on real case studies

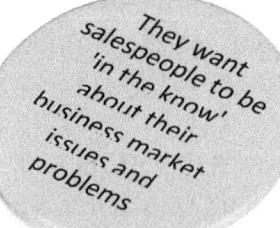

They want you to respect their time by not asking the questions that you could find the answers to by doing research.

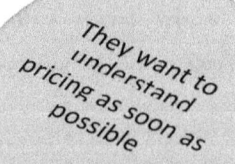

Salespeople have been programmed to hold off discussions on price for as long as possible.

The customers believe this to be a waste of time! If they are going to buy it, they will buy it

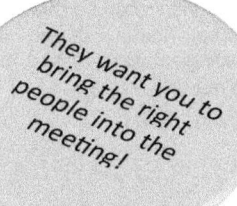

Customers complain that salespeople make the mistake of bringing too many people or the wrong people into meetings.

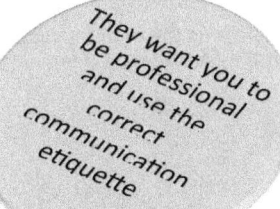

They want a formal vs casual approach, especially early in the approach.

They do not want to be treated like your college buddies: dont call them 'Dude'! And do not rely on email communication: they want you to 'talk' to them!

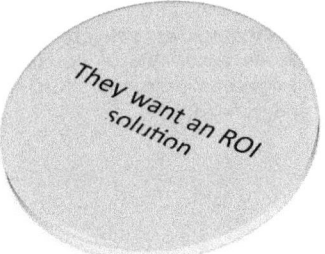

The solution that you offer had better be based on a Value Based Solution.

If it can't provide for a return for the investment, don't bother!

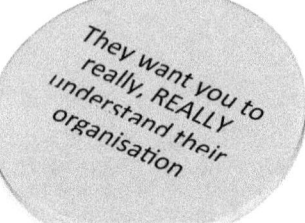

Customers say that: what really separates the great sales people from the mediocre ones are those that had clearly done their homework and had cusomised apresentation based on their specific needs.

(Death by PowerPoint)

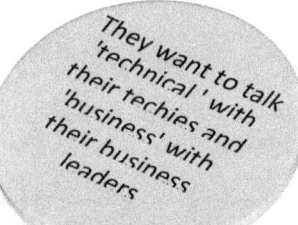

This means: talking the right language at the right time to the right people.

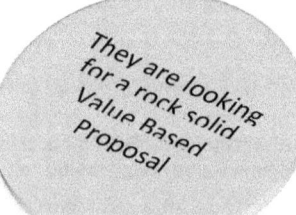

This means that you are going to have to create the awareness of potenial Shared Value Outcomes (SVOs) within your presentation.

It seems obvious from this survey that Fortune 500 customers want a 'no nonsense approach' that has to demonstrate a Value Based Proposition and a documented return for their investment; a real demonstrable ROI!

It is also very clear that they want benchmarking data. They want to measure themselves against their competition. What better way to gain access to a new customer than by asking them: "do they want to participate in a benchmarking survey?" You're not trying to sell anything to them; you are offering them a unique opportunity to benchmark their organisation. It's a real easy way to open doors!

What's in it for you? Well, what would you do if 58% of the respondents gave the same answer regarding a current challenge that they are all facing in an arena in which you specialise?

Please don't tell me this is not the easiest way to fill your pipeline with potential business! If you survey 20 customers in the same industry, and if they all have the same problems: that equals 20 real opportunities!

If you could come up with a value based proposition for their challenge, you can sell multiple solutions to the entire market segment, **OVERNIGHT!**

The benchmarking survey approach is one of the most successful ways to gain entry into a new customer's organisation or into new market segment. The customer is willing to participate because it costs them nothing and they receive valuable benchmarking data for their effort.

The challenge is: what questions will you ask?

If you ask questions that are obviously geared to leverage your position with them, or are too product related they will throw you out very quickly! The key is to disguise your product or solution based capabilities by asking the customer about what challenges they are facing! It's not a hard stretch to imagine that in any process based business the customer is facing challenges in maximising production, yield, minimising water usage, energy consumption and carbon footprint! If we focus on these areas we may come up with some opportunities.

Let me give you a few examples:

If I was in the IT business I could ask:

What is the average lost opportunity cost when you have a failure in your main servers?

How many of these failures are due to heat load in the racking system?

What's the biggest challenge you are facing when you consider now, new and future technology?

What is the average cost of server down-time in your organisation?

What is the most time consuming process that you have in machine time?

What is the most expensive process that you run through your servers?

What costs you the most money?

What makes you the most money?

What's the average time to repair? (MTTR)

What's the mean time between failures? (MTBF)

If you make the questions too product specific they will immediately realise that you are conducting a product survey, but if you're careful and keep your questions generic and focus on the Money, you will pick up all the research you need, including the costs that you need in order to calculate your value based proposition!

All you need to do is set up a date to present the survey findings and slip in your valued based proposition at the end, based on the benchmarking data. The ROI is easy to calculate once you have identified their cost structures!

In the last few years I have initiated this survey approach with many of my customers with fantastic results. The knowledge that the solutions you provide to this specific market segment have value as seen from the customer's point of view is the key: the more you sell, the more case studies you have, and the easier it is to calibrate your organisation's success factors!

Once you have concluded a specific market survey and secured the business, this is the platform that you use to initiate your CRM and the framework agreement programme with your new customers!

This is a generic flow chart depicting the survey sales process. The term APS refers to the Account Pursuit Strategy Plan. It's your value based proposition strategy document where you draft your proposal based on the survey results! (I'm going to give you this strategy breakdown after this section.)

The reference to 'start again,' of course refers to your team starting another survey approach to a different market segment. If the whole process takes 3 months then you can survey 4 specific market segments per year!

This sales strategy will facilitate multiple specific market related opportunities where your sales team can focus their energies on one or two value based propositions that can result in multiple orders every three months.

This is an organisational strategy! If you identify the market segment, the organisations and the contact people within these organisations. Create the survey questionnaire; it's then a simple task to provide each salesperson with a list of candidates to survey over a three month timeline!

The kicker is that your salespeople will only have to visit **one survey customer per week in order to achieve this!** This means that the process does not disrupt your sales team's normal routine and is easily managed.

Where does this strategy come from? Well I must admit not from me! Sun Tzu wrote a book some 2300 years ago entitled **'The Art of War'**. He had a good marketing mind when it came to the rules of engagement with his enemies; let me show you what I mean:

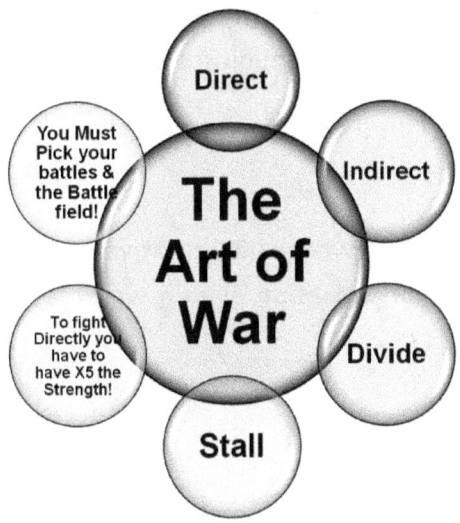

Sun Tzu tells us you can fight an enemy in one of four ways, directly, indirectly, you can stall them and you can divide them. To fight an enemy directly (your competitors in your market place) you have to have five times their strength!

This is rarely the case! I can bet you that you don't have five times the sales force of your competitor or five times the pricing advantage or five times the advertising budget!

Under these circumstances Sun Tzu would tell you to divide your enemies strength (Go all out to capture a single market segment) **divide the market!**

Don't try to fight your competitor in every market at once. You don't have enough strength!

YOU HAVE TO PICK YOUR BATTLES AND THE BATTLEFIELD!

Let me show you what this initiative can provide for you and your organisation even if we accept a terrible hit rate of only 12%.

As can be seen from the above graphic with a sales team of 5 you can run 4 surveys per year and even given the pathetic hit rate of 12% you can secure 28 new deals. If you have 15 sales people you can survey over 720 customers a year and secure 86 new deals!

In reality I can tell you this sales approach results in far greater success than 12% and has propelled some of my client's business into a new dimension.

In one such case, one of my clients has increased their sales revenue in one region by a factor of 3 in just 12 months by securing 4 additional strategic customers using this approach, combined with a 3- year framework agreement proposal!

There's nothing like presenting a value based proposition when you know what the customer wants!

If you are successful in selling it to one of them, they all want it, as peer pressure and market competition dictates the customer does not want to be left behind by their peers.

Some of you by now will be thinking why would the customer be prepared to share these strategic details with your organisation surely that represents a huge risk to them? Well not if you take a simple confidentiality and non-disclosure document with you for you and the customer to sign before you ask the survey questions!

You must protect their I.P. and they will be more open with you if they know their specific information will not be given to their competitors, especially by name! Remember you will only report back on trends and the statistics resulting from your survey.

This feedback presentation should document the questions as asked in the survey and show charts, graphics and pie chart feedback data!

You need to draw conclusions regarding the main trends and results which draw the customer to the logical solution that you will eventually propose!

The further you get into the disclosure process with the list of survey customers, the more compelling your argument can become, as you can make reference to other organisations in the segment as having bought into your solution already! There is nothing like competitive peer pressure to sell!

In one such survey, one of my customers in Texas, unearthed an opportunity in the offshore exploration drilling business. They found many surveyed customers suffering from the same problem that they didn't know existed, taking this information back to their parent organisation in Europe they found they already had a solution designed and sold in the North Sea Oil platforms.

They offered the biggest customer they surveyed a joint venture in the form of a framework agreement in order to develop a product solution for their specific challenge! Currently they have approximately $350

Million worth of solid enquiries, from this market segment, for the product **and it's not even finished yet!**

The survey approach is one relatively quick way to calibrate a successful value based proposition. Remember: once you have sold your solution to the customer you have the opportunity to hand them over to your Pharmaceutical Market Account Manager, introduce them to all of your capabilities and redirect your sales team to another market segment opportunity!

Before your competitors can react to your strategy in one market segment, you have captured market share and moved on. Fighting them indirectly, if they're not there how can they fight? Where will you strike next?

But how do you build your market or customer business pursuit strategy once you have completed your benchmarking survey?

What elements do you need to consider?

What follows is a complete breakdown of an account pursuit strategy plan. This strategy plan is generic and can be used to build strategy for any customer pursuit or, in this case, after completion of the benchmarking survey to build your market attack strategy!

It's the third strategy tool in our Combat Zone Arsenal!

Not all the elements of the plan may be relevant in every scenario but I have made it as comprehensive as possible to cover all the contingencies.

In the breakdown you will see references made to the Technical Client Review Process (TCR): this is a tactic that can really pay off if you are in direct competition for a project award!

The concept is:

Once you receive the customer's request for a quotation, you then set up a meeting to confirm your understanding of their exact needs before you propose anything! You can make the excuse that there are some small ambiguities that you need to clear up before you bid! This TCR provides you with an opportunity to upstage and outmanoeuvre your opponent by advising the customer of alternatives and optional solutions before you bid! It's a great tactic to change the goal posts before you put pen to paper!

We'll cover this tactic in more detail later. Let's look at the Pursuit Strategy Plan in detail:

The account pursuit strategy plan

The plan below includes for a customer presentation plan. I will cover this section of strategy when we look at the framework agreement plan in detail later in the book.

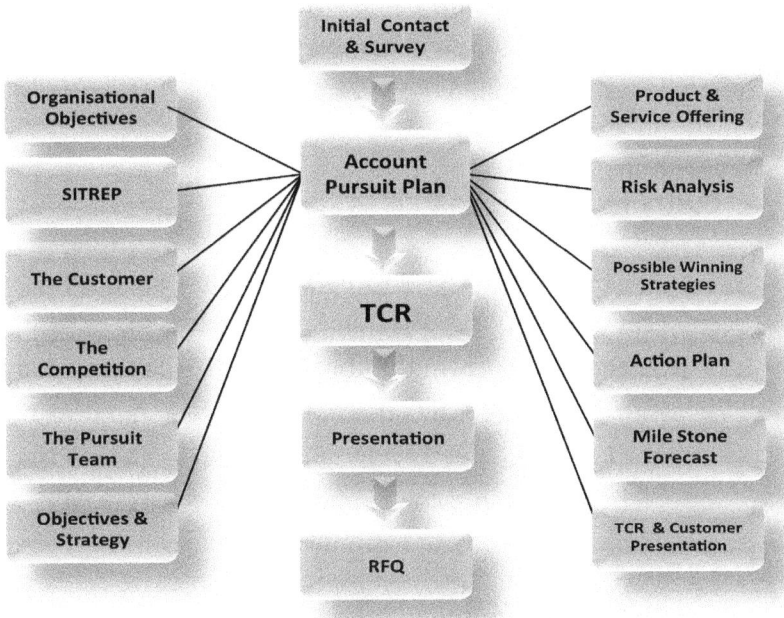

The above model is a generic plan for an account Pursuit Strategy document.

The Structure of the plan should encompass the following elements:

Contents and compliance

The first section of your account pursuit plan should have a Content and compliance sheet detailing all the relevant sections of the plan, when they were completed and a signature of who compiled them.

Customer Registration

The next section should contain a simple Customer registration page detailing all the relevant customer information, the date the plan was initiated and the date the plans need to be completed for review and mandate to proceed by the senior Management.

The Account Pursuit Plan Model

The next section should contain a plan model as suggested above for reorientation and team discussion.

Survey Results

The section following the pursuit plan model should contain the survey questions and the customer responses to the questionnaire for reference. In the case of a specific market segment survey the compiled data and any resultant trends or similarities need to be documented here!

The Organisational Objectives

This is where the pursuit team documents what they want to achieve with this customer or market segment. It's the empty canvass so to speak! It documents what the team anticipates the segment or customer's potential for business is. The types of solutions or products the customer is capable of buying and the size of the prize! It also contains the phased approach or potential timing to reach the segment / customer's full potential.

The SITREP (the current situation)

In this section the pursuit team documents the current situation existing with the customer or market segment.

The competitive situation, current products and services they are using, the current relationships that exist and any compelling events arising from the survey questionnaire conducted with the customer. In short, this is an executive overview of the customer's situation at present regarding your discipline, product or service offerings.

The Customer Analysis

This section of the plan details the structure and complexity of the customers business. This part can get complex if you are building strategy for a market segment as you may have to document multiple customer profiles. This is where you need a team to share the workload.

How do the customers make buying decisions? How do they adjudicate tenders, how vertically or horizontally complex is their management structure? Who are the decision makers?

It is important to document the process the customer adopts to purchase products and services through their supply chain.

It is essential to know whether entry at head office level will guarantee business in all of their business units or affiliates or whether this decision making is a decentralised function within their group!

In addition it is important to document whether the customer is suffering from any specific organisational challenges such as:

Space limitations,
Storage limitations,
Finance limitations,
Experience limitations,
Budget limitations,
Standardisation limitations,
Labour limitations,
Timing limitations,
Legal limitations.

The most important aspect of the research is discovering any common compelling events that the customer or market segment will have to react to!

New environmental legislation, impending energy cost increases, water restrictions, expansions, mergers and acquisitions. You get the picture, and these compelling events can provide you with the opportunity you need to win their business.

Finally, it is important to document what the customer thinks they need and what they want! These are two different things! The pursuit team needs to document what they know the customer needs and the needs the customer is currently unaware of!

Competition

In this section of the plan the pursuit team needs to document as much information as possible on the current competitors the customer is using.

Their strengths and weaknesses compared to your organisation, the length of tenure, relationships that exist and if possible an estimation of the size of the business they currently enjoy from the customer.

It would also help if you could understand their pricing policy and cost structures.

The most important element of this information is where are your competitor's weaknesses?

In short what are you up against in trying to gain entry to this business?

The Pursuit Team

At this point in your pursuit plan you should be in a strong position to determine the kind of team you are going to need to gain entry to this business.

Who are the potential candidates that should make up the pursuit team?

Who do you need to gain entry to this business?

Why do you need them and what special disciplines or experience is needed, who in senior management do you need to influence the customer's executive?

How many people do you need and when?

By documenting the justification for your 'dream team' helps in clarifying the tactics and strategies you will use to win the business!

Objectives and Strategy

This section of your pursuit plan should identify your objectives and the team's strategies to achieve them.

Many 'blue sky' ideas can be documented here for team discussion and review by more experienced, older or senior people in your organisation. This process is essential to safeguard against errors in judgment and or gaps in the objectives strategy and ensures an organisational solution that calibrates the strategy for success.

Product and Service offering

This section of the plan details the products and service offering you intend to offer the customer/ segment.

It is essential to take into consideration the timing and a phased approach to what you intend to offer the customer in your first approach; you don't want to scare them off!

Here you document the pricing structures you believe will be needed to gain entry to the account and the value based proposition you intend to use.

Risk Analysis

At this point in the pursuit plan it is a good time to run a risk analysis of the strategy.

Have you thought of all the issues? Have you covered all the bases?

If you list the strengths and weaknesses of your plan at this point you will be able to cancel many of the perceived weaknesses out and arrive at your winning strategy. That comes next!

Possible Winning Strategy

After conducting the risk analysis with your team you should be in a strong position to determine your winning strategy. This section of your pursuit plan documents the culmination of your teams thought process in gaining entry to this customer's business. Determine the step by step process you are going to use to achieve this strategy and its objectives.

The Action Plan

The next step is to develop you detailed action plan.

Objectives, people, actions, time-frames and the collateral you will need to accomplish your goals.

The Milestone Plan

A mile stone plan is different to an action plan as is concentrates the teams attention and focus on achieving progress milestones. In a way it focuses the team on achieving critical path objectives by a certain date to keep the action plan on track. I seriously recommend you consider this step in your pursuit plan as it rewards the team for achieving goals not calendar dates!

The TCR (Technical Client Review)

At this stage of your pursuit plan it would be nice to bounce some of your strategies and assumptions off one of your customer's junior management to gauge their reaction before you go to print!

As I have stated previously in the book a TCR is a fantastic strategy to 'test the water' with any customer before you put your final presentation together. Don't formally present, simply talk big picture strategies to gauge their reaction to your approach, in this way you will be able to fine tune your final presentation to encompass all of the finer details your potential customer requires.

The best person to do this with is the person you conducted the initial survey questionnaire with; they will give you the feedback you need. All you have to do now is set the date for the executive presentation to senior management and you have achieved your platform to present your valued based proposition.

So in this section of the plan, document who you want to run the TCR with and who from your team will you need to achieve this milestone objective?

The Final Customer Presentation

I have detailed the presentation plan in the
Framework Agreement section of the book, page
161 for your reference.

This plan may seem very detailed and a considerable
amount of work and you would be right! However, how
on earth are you going to capture new strategic
business without such a strategy? Simply leave it to your
sales person to come up with a comprehensive detailed
plan that has a high potential to be successful? You
could, but not on my team!

**Less than 10% of sales organisations I have had the
pleasure of dealing with over the last 18 years have
had anything approaching this strategic customer
centric strategy approach to securing new business.
That's why they find it so hard to secure new business,
they don't have a strategy!!**

Chapter Summary:

- To successfully break into a new customer or market segment you need to consider the benchmarking survey approach.
- Pick a specific market segment that uses your product or service offering.
- Formulate no more than 20 generic questions.
- Invite the customer to participate based on the fact you will share the results with them.
- Sign a confidentiality agreement with them to protect their I.P.
- Over a three month period run the survey
- Each sales person in a team of 5 needs to see one survey customer a week.
- At the end of the three months correlate the answers.
- Look for the most common Data and any specific opportunities.
- Look for any compelling events.
- Build your account pursuit strategy and your value based proposition based on the findings.
- Build a presentation revealing the results of the survey and add your value based proposition based on the findings.

- Formalise your offer by way of a written proposal or framework agreement proposal.
- Focus the sales team on another market segment for the next 3 months

- **Review your hit rate. Measure your pipeline and Count your Money!!!**

4.

Customer Relationship Management (CRM)

Now that you have a new customer, what are you going to do with them? What is CRM or strategic account management going to do for this new relationship? Let's review the advantages of this, the third initiative in this book.

Strategic account management or CRM is the management of a strategic customer's business by a professional dedicated, small team of your people to maximise the return on investment, minimise risk and maximise the probability of continued growth and sustainable value generation for both stakeholders.

It is the perfect platform, managed correctly, to continually sell up and sell forward for any sales organisation! In many ways it is the perfect solution for retaining the customer's continued business while blocking any attempts by your competition to gain entry.

Having said all that: why is it so successful and why is the customer so inclined to welcome this approach?

To fully understand the case for CRM we need to start by understanding the benefits that CRM can provide for your organisation and theirs.

When people talk about CRM they are generally talking about software tracking system, designed to act as a real time database for the sales organisation. The system tracks sales calls and trends and makes specific correlations between like customers and your business with them.

That's not the CRM I'm referring to here!

What I'm referring to is a management plan; a strategic account development plan and a jointly developed alignment process detailing how the two organisations will do business and measure the success of the joint venture. I first made mention of this alignment process in my first book back in 1999. It appears that this process is becoming even more essential in our modern day business dealings.

To keep your finger successfully on the pulse of any substantial customer business, you have to see them face-to-face! You have to see senior managers and not just the guys on the shop floor. We have to have access to their operational people! This is not easy! And unless you have an agreed to plan, you won't see them for months at a time! **THAT'S NOT MANAGING YOUR BUSINESS!**

Sending your sales guy in every three weeks to ask their contact at the shop floor level whether or not everything is alright; and do they have anymore work for you, is simply not enough! If we want to have an in-depth mutually beneficial relationship with our customers, we are going to have to make one!

So let's make the case for CRM!

These 2 graphics detail some of the benefits that CRM can provide your organisation.

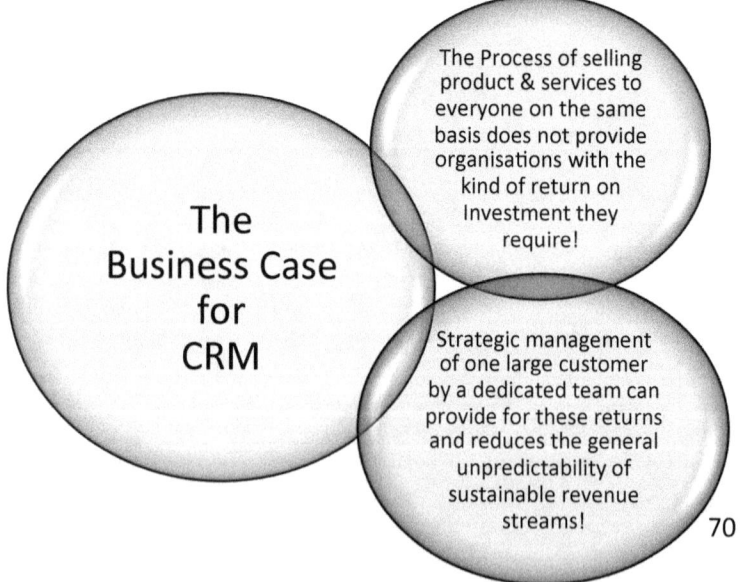

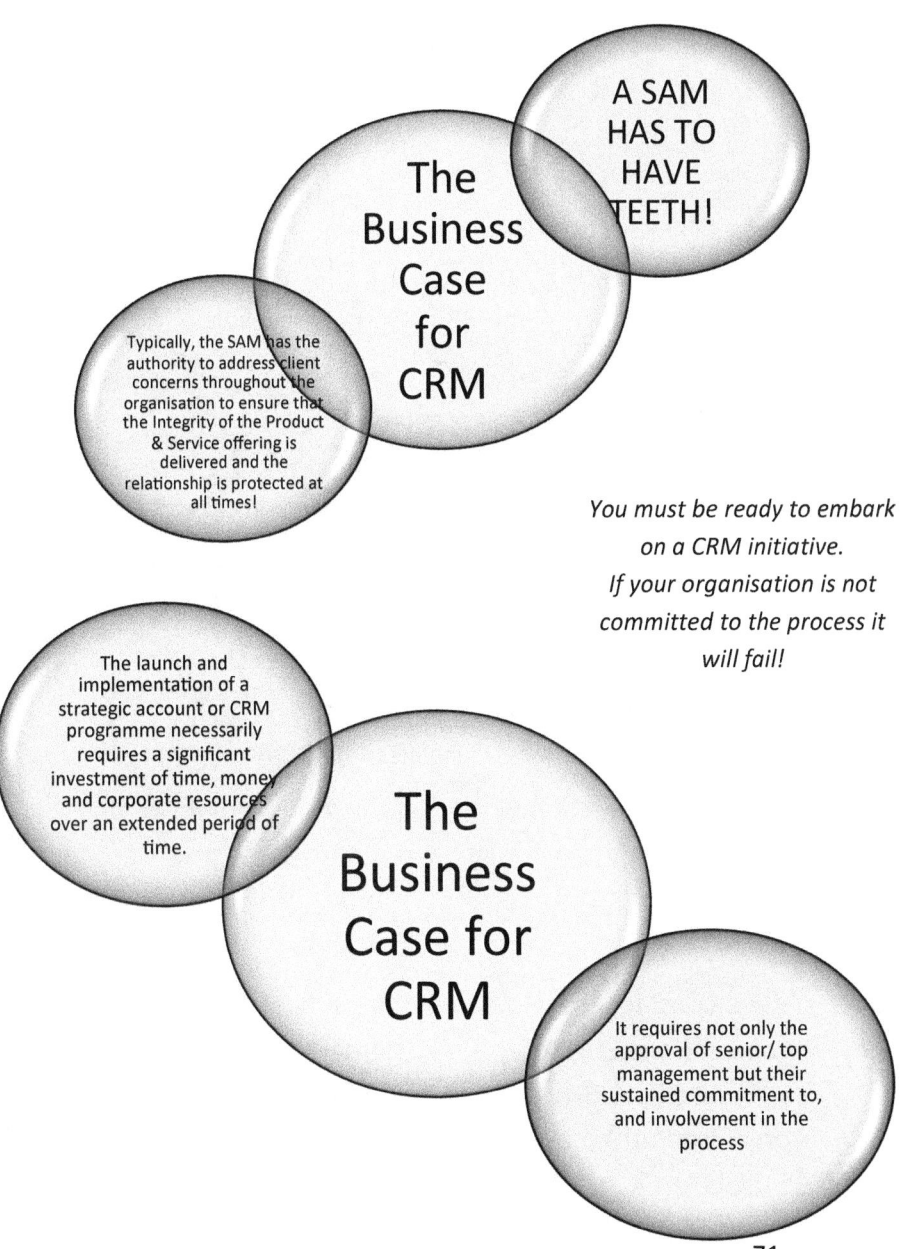

A SAM HAS TO HAVE TEETH!

The Business Case for CRM

Typically, the SAM has the authority to address client concerns throughout the organisation to ensure that the Integrity of the Product & Service offering is delivered and the relationship is protected at all times!

You must be ready to embark on a CRM initiative. If your organisation is not committed to the process it will fail!

The launch and implementation of a strategic account or CRM programme necessarily requires a significant investment of time, money and corporate resources over an extended period of time.

The Business Case for CRM

It requires not only the approval of senior/ top management but their sustained commitment to, and involvement in the process

This graphic lists the organisational benefits one can derive from a CRM strategy.

If we consider the old adage that 80% of your business comes from 20% of your customers, imagine what a structured CRM Programme will do for your organisation! You will be able to structure this business with fewer resources and maximise your returns on this Investment! Your budgeting process become easy, you considerably reduce the risk of doing business and increase the probability of sustainable and profitable business for your shareholders.

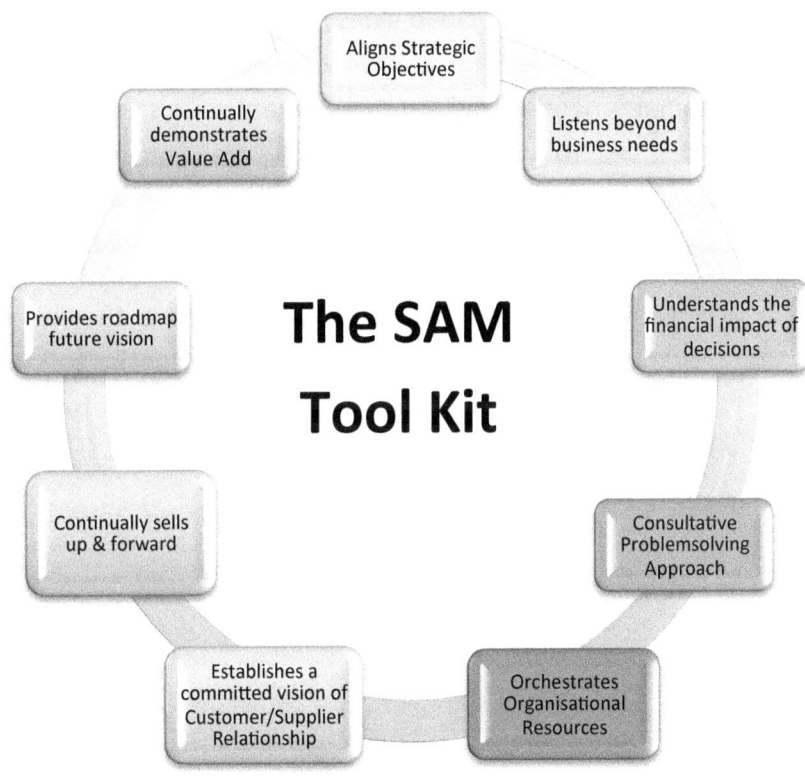

The above graphic depicts some of the specialised skills the strategic account manager needs to manage a sophisticated customer.

Strategic account managers do not grow on trees; you have to obtain them or train them but a word of warning, don't try and turn one of your best salespeople into a SAM! You need to keep your best sales people to sell new business! Good sales people are not cut out for this management role! A SAM needs to be a business manager/leader and a team player; your sales people are used to working alone, they are aggressive and tenacious; in addition they generally are not viewed by the rest of the organisation as senior management.

If you try this, it will fail, you will lose the sales revenue these salespeople normally bring in to the organisation and you will lose a valuable sales person in the process!

Some of the overriding benefits of a CRM Programme are as follows:

- For your account Managers. Due to the nature of the routine operational meetings with the customer, they will in general get one month to report back and not 3 times a day!
- The everyday phone calls from the customers are greatly reduced as they know you have structured meetings and a reporting structure to follow.
- Phone bills are cut in half as your sales people do not have to constantly phone the customer back to provide feedback and the day-to-day problem solving activities normally associated with managing a strategic customer.
- Saving in fuel bills! Customer visits are reduced.
- Your account manager get's to see all of the important people from the customer at one time, in one meeting.
- In general, the customer hands over work to be done once a month and your account manager saves the time, effort and expense of driving to the customer's facility 3 times a month!

- No appointments need to be made. They are set!
- You can plan your organisational resources more efficiently.
- You can forecast 80% of your sales budget with these customer's with high accuracy.
- You can increase the probability of sustainable and profitable business.
- You can maximise your ROI.
- You can achieve more profitable revenue streams with fewer people.
- You can retain market share.
- You can increase the barriers of entry for any competitor.
- You can continually demonstrate and record your value based proposition to the customer.
- You can use this success story, in the form of case studies, to help you secure further business.

- **You can calibrate your business for success!**

I like to think of a CRM Agreement as:

'The glue between the two'

You will know when your CRM plan is working. The customer will start asking you to take responsibility for more and more business opportunities between your two organisations. You may have to grow your business into areas you never thought possible to keep up with their demands!

So if we have managed to sell you the case for initiating a CRM Programme with your strategic customers the next step is to show you what a typical CRM Plan looks like and what information needs to be agreed on and documented between you and your customer!

A Customer Relationship Management Plan

Joint Mission Statement

Business Objectives

Strategic Opportunities

Governance

Operational Reviews

Scope Definition

You

CRM

Customer

Change Controls

Product & Service Definition

Quality Control

Relationship Integrity

SVO'S & KPI'S

Documentation Protocol

The joint mission statement:

To cement any business relationship, there's nothing like a joint mission statement to keep everyone on track. Take this part seriously, as when they start shouting at you in 12 months time you can simply refer to the mission statement to shut them up and focus on the big picture!

The business objectives:

The next part of your plan should be to agree and document the business objectives of the relationship. It helps to prioritise these objectives and assign them a weighting and timetable if possible.

Strategic Opportunities:

What's happening in the next three months? What urgent or compelling events are taking place within your customer's organisation that represents tactical or strategic importance to your customer?

These opportunities can be discussed and documented for immediate implementation. Don't be surprised if the customer wants you to do work for them immediately, it may be one of the reasons they decide to take up your offer!

Under normal circumstances, It helps to define these strategic issues in as much detail as possible, define the desired outcomes and attach monetary values to them if and when they are secured.

To help in your implementation plan you should attempt to schedule these strategic goals for completion every quarter i.e. first 3 Months, 6 months, 9 months and 12 months targets.

Governance:

In all businesses today, the importance of good corporate citizenship, transparent dealings and adherence to legal and financial governance is essential. You need to discuss and document all necessary policies and procedures required to protect your customer and yourselves during this business relationship.

Operational Reviews:

This is where your SAM team saves huge time and money for your organisation. This is where you agree with the customer where, when and how often you will meet to measure and report on the operational aspects of the relationship.

This is where you document who will attend these meetings and agree on a provisional agenda to be followed. It is at these operational reviews when you get the chance to report on the progress to date on the relationship objectives, strategic goals and any measurable KPI'S or SVO's (known performance indices

& shared value outcomes) this is where you get the chance to brag about the results your CRM plan has achieved (Remember the black suit!) Your sales team can sell up and sell forward and advise the client on your forthcoming plans and objectives.

These meetings provide a perfect platform to present future product road maps, additional offerings and talk financial planning or capex on the customer's part to secure these offerings into your customer's portfolio.

These meetings, based on the specific customer and or industry can be monthly, quarterly or every 6 months. Whatever is decided, it is essential that you agree on a specific rule set for these meetings i.e. the last Friday of every month, the last Friday of each quarter, whatever is decided and agreed, document the specific dates and lock them in concrete at this CRM planning meeting.

If you don't they will never happen and all this work will be for nothing!

Scope Definition:

It is essential at this CRM planning meeting that you define the exact scope of your offering to the customer and they define their expectations of your organisation.

All parties must be absolutely clear of the deliverables and responsibilities of each party before the CRM process begins. This greatly simplify matters as this relationship goes forward as it identifies original scope and any additional work can be easily identified and accepted as such by the customer. This brings us to change controls.

Change Controls:

As stated above, be very careful to define the exact scope of your initial offering as customers are notorious for scope creep after a contract is signed. If you're not careful you will be doing a lot of extra work for your strategic partner for free! This is where change controls come in!

Once original scope is defined and agreed you will have to discuss, agree and document a change control procedure. If and when you are instructed or requested to perform any additional work above and or beyond the original defined scope, this procedure needs to detail the people, the methodology and when these changes to scope will be sanctioned and paid for!

This is an extremely important part of your CRM plan. Get this wrong at the beginning and you may find yourself in trouble with your customer real quick!

Product and Service Definition:

This is different from the scope definition, which primarily details responsibilities and deliverables under the contract. This is where you agree and document the details of your list of products and or services you will provide the customer under this contract or framework agreement. It defines the exact products, their model no's, part No's and service definitions.

This is a perfect time to immediately try to sell up and add additional products and services to the customer right from the get go! You're entering into a strategic relationship right? Where's the harm in trying to twist their arms on you supplying a little extra service for a little extra cash? You won't get anything unless you try, right!

Quality Control:

Almost all organisations competing in our global market place are ISO Compliant. That means they have a documented quality control procedure you must adhere to! You need to discuss, agree and document any special procedures you may have to comply with to undertake this business with them!

Relationship Integrity:

How are you going to measure the wellbeing of the relationship?

This is a difficult area; however it is essential if you are going to circumvent any relationship problems in the future. What if you have a fall out over an important issue? What if you disagree strongly about a decision your customer will make! How are you going to resolve these issues? This part of your plan needs to document a procedure that either provides for conflict resolution or arbitration.

In many instances the simple solution is to nominate senior management from both organisations to resolve the situation to the mutual satisfaction of both parties. These procedures are generally documented and catered for within the commercial terms and conditions of the customer, read them, if you're in agreement with them simply make reference to them in your CRM plan and get your customer to agree with the process. They should have no problem it's their T & Cs after all!

SVOs and KPIs:

Shared Value Outcomes (SVO) and soft and hard known performance indices (KPI). These are the performance measurements your value based proposition will be measured by! Don't be afraid to set 4 or 5 measurements especially shared value outcomes because as the phrase alludes to these are measurements that can benefit both parties! What if you can set an SVO around a financial target where if the target is reached both parties share in the financial gain? That would be one I'm sure you would want to sign!

Remember the black suit! You want to be measured on performance but don't get too fancy. Never let your mouth write a cheque your body can't cash! Keep these measurements as simple as possible; at least to start with. You can always get a little more ambitious once you get your feet under the table!

Documentation Protocol:

The last thing you need to document in your CRM plan is the agreed to documentation protocol. Who sees what, how many copies, in what media and who signs for what and when!

The CRM strategy agreement

If you have a standard customer heads of agreement this is where you include it in your offer. They rarely sign it but it's there to show you are serious about your offer and prepared to put your organisation on the line regarding the responsibilities contained within the agreement.

That's it! That's your CRM plan. All you have to do now is live by its rules and procedures and deliver on your promises! That is how you maximise your sales dollar, return on investment and create sustainable business returns with your strategic partners. Good luck!

The next step in our journey is combining this process with a much more far reaching initiative of the strategic framework agreement

Chapter summary

The CRM plan consists of discussing, agreeing upon and documenting the following strategic parameters with your customer:

- A joint mission statement.
- Business objectives.
- Strategic opportunities.
- Governance.
- Operational reviews.
- Scope definition.
- Change controls.
- Product & service definition.
- Quality control.
- Relationship integrity.
- SVO's and KPI's
- Documentation protocol.

The advantages of you creating a customer relationship management plan with a strategic customer will have many spin-off benefits to your organisation that are not generally recognised on face value!

Let's now explore the fourth initiative in this book. The, the open framework agreement proposal!

5.

The Framework Agreement:

What is a non-exclusive framework agreement proposal?

Apart from your most effective weapon you can use against a competitor, who is strongly positioned in a customer you want to do business with, it is a non-threatening, powerful tool to gain entry via a company's supply chain because it can circumvent the normal pre-qualification and bidding process and short track your organisation to secure business, long term business, from your targeted customer!

This is a proactive and pre-emptive strike sales initiative!

The customer has not solicited this offer from your organisation; you have chosen to provide them this offer by your own free will in the pursuit of gaining entry to their business!

This offer, unsolicited, will allow them to open up the negotiation game!

Corporate governance in any organisational supply chain can seriously limit an organisation's ability to continuously test the market for competitive pricing.

Once they have issued a request for quotation (RFQ), the adjudication of such tenders, the negotiation process and eventual order award to the successful bidder takes months (can be as long as 12 months) and at each stage is strictly governed by their forensic policies and procedures. **(For more on this supply chain process, see 'Do Nothing Negotiation'.)**

The problem is, they are constantly under pressure to reduce costs and increase the performance levels of their current service providers and once an order is placed, there is only so much pressure they can bring to bear due to the contract in place! So, if they feel they have an underperforming suppliers **or they are suddenly presented with a better or more comprehensive offer that has no strings attached, this upsets the apple cart in a big way!**

Remember the framework agreement offer I am suggesting is a non-exclusive offer! It just says if you do business with us, this is our value based proposition and this is how we will conduct and manage the relationship!

You are not demanding they give you all of their business; it's entirely up to them! If you try to pitch an exclusive deal you won't get far today, no modern organisational supply chain is ever going to put all of their eggs in one basket. Exclusive single source supply is too risky! A non-exclusive offer is a non-threatening approach; you potential customer has no reason not to look at it and take your offer seriously.

Who should attempt to make this offer to your strategically targeted customer?

This is where we need to explain some of the compelling reasons why this initiative can be so successful for any sales organisation.

It constitutes the very heart of the growing trend in fortune 100 companies to return to the initiatives used during the 1970,s of proposing business to business business (BBB)

It has been reported; in various studies conducted during 2013 that approximately 18% to 20% of all the business conducted in the fortune 100 during that year was based on a BBB approach!

This is very significant, as this initiative represents a fundamental shift in the way large corporations are conducting business!

This is not a sales driven initiative; it's an organisational driven strategy! The normal sales approach with its associated sales cycle and associated competitive roadblocks are circumvented!

In my experience over the last two years with the organisations that I have worked with on this initiative the sales department has had very little to do with this strategic direction at all, except for their involvement in choosing the targeted corporate and presenting the offer to the customer. It has been driven by the organisations executive!

This I believe is being driven by the recognition that the traditional way organisations have sold their products and services to their customers no longer provide them with the returns on investment they require to survive! Whereas corporate business doing business with corporate business does!

This is a little scary to me as in 1999, in my first book Selling in the 21st Century I predicted the death of the sales division in most traditional businesses due to the way global businesses will strategically view the economics, financial costs and logistical challenges they face when relying on their sale teams to capture sufficiently large and sustainable business. It's fast becoming obvious that this can only be achieved by the organisations top executives, organisation to organisation!

The average sales team is out of their depth when it comes to these initiatives and that is why the framework agreement offer provides sales organisations with a strategic tool to facilitate this rapid and game changing shift in corporate business!

Let me outline some of the most obvious reasons why these BBB framework agreement proposals are so successful

- The framework agreement does not rely on the skills of any sales person to gain entry to any another corporate business.
- These initiatives are driven by the executive who are more experienced and skilled to operate at this corporate level.
- The targeting of these potential corporate customers is made at the executive level based on sustainable returns on investment, not opportunistic periodic business.

- Long term framework agreements are targeted at capturing large business revenues with high probabilities of sustainable profit.
- Framework agreements reduce the dependence on sales organisations having to capture large amounts of small business to achieve sales targets.
- Corporate framework agreements circumvent the need to prequalify and bid for a customer's business.
- They have the effect of a pre-emptive strike on the sales organisation's competitors.
- The global challenge of constantly competing for every scrap of business with every customer is not sustainable.
- Long term framework agreements increase the barriers of entry for any competitor.
- Framework agreements greatly increase the potential for customer retention.
- Organisations supply chain trends are advocating the reduction in multiple supplier dependence.
- Corporate supply chain trends indicate framework agreements (BBB) reduces risk and provides for better economies of scale.
- Corporate BBB reduces the need to go to the market for competitive tenders.

- Sales organisations can offer better economies of scale for guaranteed long term business.
- The opportunity that framework agreements (BBB) provide for in creating robust and mutually beneficial corporate relationships cannot be underestimated.

That is why, at this point I must point out that any offer of this nature must be made at a customer's head office level.

You are going to have to approach the supply chain head of the particular tower handling your products or service offerings or even the executive level to get results!

Any attempt to gain entry at any operating level or site locations may be thwarted by local allegiances to the current service supplier or worse, they have no executive clout to make a decision!

If you make your unsolicited offer at head office level this gives the overall supply chain head a legitimate reason to enter into an exploratory process to determine, if indeed, they are getting the best deal from their current supplier and more importantly if your framework offer is more comprehensive and offers more value based return on their investment **they are**

forced by their own governance to explore the opportunity to its fullest extent!

You may ask how they can do this when they have a current contract in place with another supplier. Well here's the kicker. If your offer includes for things they want and the current supplier has not offered that in their current contract or you offer a rebate structure on yearly order volumes received and they don't, this changes the ball game and allows them to open up the competition again! **Your framework offer is based on a 3 year contract!**

They may go out for tender to give their current supplier the opportunity to re quote their offer based on 3 years work and or encompass the new elements you have offered in your proposal.

They may issue an offer for suppliers to submit 'an expression of interest' for this all encompassing 3 year contract. This doesn't mean they will stop doing business with their current supplier, but based on the contract in place they may choose to split the business between two suppliers or wait until the current 1 year contract runs out and change horses entirely!

"Hold on" I hear you say! Go out on tender to encompass the new elements you have offered in your proposal? That's not right!

Well it will happen to you if you do not protect your intellectual property. That is why it is **essential** for you to encompass a non-disclosure, confidentiality agreement in your framework agreement before you present your deal!

This will stop the customer using your framework agreement offer as a template for any enquiry they may wish to issue resulting from your offer.

This makes it very difficult for any other competitor to match your offer. **They don't know what they don't know!** The only thing the customer can do is allude to 'all encompassing,' fully comprehensive' and other descriptors to entice the current supplier or any other interesting party to offer the same deal as you. **But they cannot be explicit!**

Having said all this, if your 3 year non-exclusive framework agreement proposal is more expensive than the customer's current supplier, then I'm afraid you have wasted your time!

How can we make sure our offer is more attractive than our competitors?

We need to study the customer business, how do they make their money? How do they operate? We are going to have to consider many elements of our framework agreement offer to come up with some real tangible value based propositions they cannot afford to ignore! Let's explore some options we can use.

We can use an old Sprat to catch a Mackerel! **Phased in pricing!**

Every one of us who has been in business for any length of time will be able to gauge their competitor's position of strength compared to their own. This includes market related pricing and their respective capabilities.

The process we are exploring is not for sissies! This is serious business. If your company could gain access to 3 years work from a new customer what is that worth?

If we consider the possibility that this framework agreement acts like **'The glue between the two'** you may secure this companies business way into the future, put a price on that? So how attractive are you going to make your framework proposal?

You will only get one shot at this so your offer must be streets ahead of your competition! What are your options? Let me give you some suggestions:

Planning for this initiative is essential. (That's why a strategic Pursuit plan is essential) It starts at budget time! You must budget for this initiative. Let's say you want to offer phased in pricing for the first year of your 3 year framework agreement. Let's for argument sake say you want to pitch your first year pricing 15% lower than your normal selling price to ensure entry to the business, you are going to have to make a provision in your balance sheet to make up for this loss in operating profit in the 1st year of trading!

You can't survive selling at less 15%. It will kill you. So, you must find the money somewhere! Less golf with your current customers, no fancy exhibition this year, **I don't care where you find the money, just find it!**

At the end of the year you can take this budget provision and prop up the margin you have achieved from the new business initiative so you're overall plan and your ROI reaches target!

You can phase in your normal pricing in the second year based on your performance in the first. This a reasonable approach and if you offer a rebate structure based on business received in year 1, 2 and 3 you can soften the blow to the customer while still enticing them to place the maximum business with you to secure these rebates!

Remember all rebate structures are paid yearly and are generally paid based on a sliding scale, separately calculated from business volume based milestones. **They are not cumulative!**

If you do your math correctly the customer should only be paying a little more than a normal inflationary price increase. Which is offset by the other value based elements of your offer.

What other value based propositions can you offer to secure this business?

Well don't forget the CRM process we explored earlier, this will form part of your framework agreement offer and you would do well to pre-empt the thought processes here before you submit your package deal.

The CRM Plan dictates who will do what, when and how it will be done! Any activity you can perform that the customer currently is responsible for represents a saving for them! You need to document these potential savings in your value based proposition.

To raise a piece of paper in a large corporate today is estimated at around $400. Any documentation you can take responsibility for is a saving for them.

Man hours. Remember the (MTTR) and (MTBF) figures we discussed earlier, well, any work you can do that saves the customer from doing it themselves is a saving for them. Based on an estimated man hour costs, document the savings you can provide them.

Any reduction or extension to the on line operating hours or reduction in repair time in the customer business is a massive saving for them. If you can calculate what this time saving represents in either the reduction of lost production time or additional production time based on their profit margins. These values will make your product or service costs pale in comparison!

You need to document every cent you can save them, or make them!

Some other value based propositions you could consider are as follows:

- A strategic product and service discount based on your price list to secure the 3 year contract.

- Additional savings based on an upfront deposit based on yearly projected volumes. I.e. less 2% for a 20% upfront payment every year during the contract. They are going to pay you anyway, right!
- Additional savings for quarterly payments paid in advance based on the same projected volumes. You could invoice them once every 3 months and conduct a quarterly recon Imagine the time saving here!
- Additional savings based on a 3 plus 2 year contract. Ostensibly a 5 year framework agreement instead of 3 years.
- An additional saving on invoices that exceed a specific value in any given quarter during the contract period. (This can aid in yearend balance sheet shortfalls)
- A yearly rebate structure (as mentioned above) based on yearly business received

In the last two years it has been my experience that the customer is more interested in reducing their risk in conducting sustainable business than they are in saving a few dollars, so yes, you're value based proposition has to be attractive but its more about your professionalism and capabilities in helping the customer in achieving their objectives than the money, they want a rock solid relationship and sustainable, predictable high performance, that's more important to them than anything.

In summary, your value based proposition, worded carefully and structured with as many value based propositions as possible will certainly put the cat amongst the pigeons and give you a straight shot at the big prize! After all, your offer is an open ended non exclusive offer what has the customer got to lose? It's Win - Win all round!

Ok, so that's the introduction to your framework agreement initiative but what should one of these proposals look like? What information should they contain and how do you structure one?

That comes next!

Chapter Summary:

An open, non exclusive framework agreement proposal is your most powerful weapon you can deploy against your competition!

- It represents a new approach to capturing large business opportunities (BBB)
- It opens up opportunities for a customer's supply chain to legitimately question the competitiveness of their current suppliers pricing structures.
- It circumvents the need to pre qualify for any business via the supply chain governance procedures.
- Unsolicited, it poses no threat to established supply chain doctrines and forensic methodologies.
- It can force an organisation to re-examine the current supplier status quo.
- It must by nature be extremely attractive commercially.
- It must contain multiple value based propositions for the customer's consideration.
- It must be comprehensive in its scope. It must contain every element of the design, supply, delivery, installation, commissioning, project

management, financial management and logistical control that the customer would demand as a strategic partnering initiative.

- It must contain performance criteria, reporting structures and lines of responsibility.
- It must contain suggested SVO's and KPI's.
- It must be structured so as it can form part of a customer contract agreement without them having to re work the document.
- It must cover all aspects of the customer's general terms and conditions.

- **It should provide the customer with a dilemma. How could they justify a decision not to take advantage of your offer?**

To truly get a sense of the complexity of such a offer, read on, in the next chapters we will spell out how to build such an offer with examples of what you can say and how to say it!

6.

The Framework Agreement Plan:

The following graphic depicts the generic contents of a framework agreement plan. In the following chapters we will take each element and describe the contents and structure in more detail.

The Framework Agreement Plan

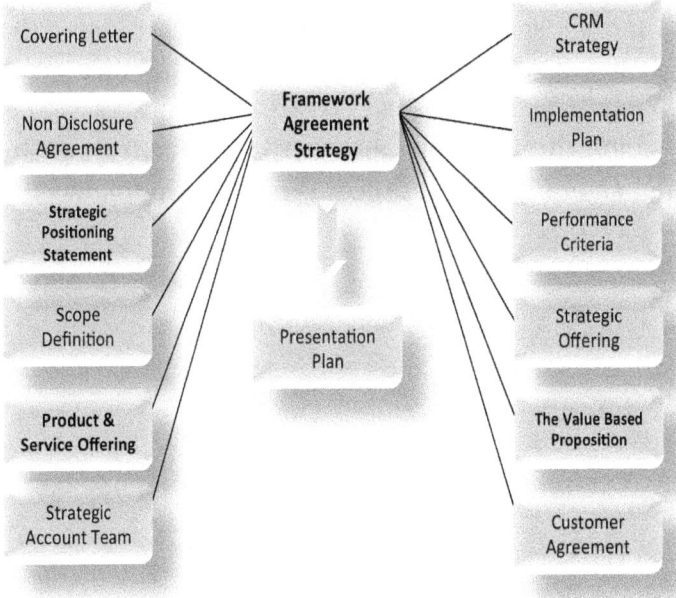

The above strategy plan contains 13 basic elements that are essential to cover in a comprehensive Framework agreement offer. They are by no means exhaustive. Your offer may want to detail alternative or additional elements based on your specific business offering. However, in my experience this model has catered for 90% of the basic structures offered by my customers, they, however, sometimes change the descriptors to better suit their culture, environment or customers.

In my business I customise these strategy documents for my clients so they sit as a team and draft out their offer before submitting them to their customers. (If you want one, just contact us by mail and I'll send you one.)

During the next few chapters I will illustrate as much as I can of the exact process you need to follow.

7.

The Covering letter:

The very first thing your customer should see when they open your Framework Agreement offer (or your positioning document) is a covering letter. Some people may prefer to call this an executive overview.

This document should of course be on a formal company letter head and signed by your most senior manager or executive. This letter legitimises the offer to your customer; it's a formal business proposal!

What should this document say? An executive overview is designed to be scanned! Very rarely do senior managers read a whole document, so an executive overview is designed to have maximum impact and maximum relevant information in the shortest possible space. Simply put, it's the what, the why and the how that's contained within the offer.

Let me give you an example:

The target Company Name.

Postal Address.

Attention. The customers full name.

Dear Mr

RE: PROPOSED STRATEGIC FRAMEWORK POSITIONING DOCUMENT

We thank you for affording us this opportunity to present this framework proposal to you and the ACME Group Team.

For some time we have considered the ACME company as an important potential strategic partner within our business. Over the last 40 years we have continuously strived to distinguish ourselves in the efficiency, timeousness and professionalism that we have shown when called upon by your industry to undertake and participate in high profile..........................projects and subsequent contracted activities.

However, in our dealings with your industry and specifically for the ACME Company in the future we have come to realise that we could be of assistance to your organisation in a far more comprehensive and productive manner in order to continuously assist you in managing these ....projects and contracts in a more cost effectively and value generating partnership if we could only *bring to bear the other specialised skills that **your company name** possess in this field of expertise.*

We believe that this is the perfect time, given the current financial environment, to inform you of our willingness to partner with your organisation and offer you a comprehensive 3 year non exclusive framework agreement to ensure the continued proactive release of value within your asset base going forward.

*The enclosed positioning document and subsequent presentation is tabled for your consideration and joint discussion to investigate any, or all, of the encompassed capabilities where **your company name** may add value to the ACME Group within this specialised arena.*

Assuring you of our best attention now and at all times in the future.

Yours sincerely

Short and sweet! I'm sure, in your own specialised field of expertise you will be able to draft a much better executive overview, however, just remember to keep it as short as possible. The most important message you want to send is that this offer is comprehensive, based on value propositions and is fully backed by your organisation's top executives.

You will notice the letter refers to a presentation that accompanies your positioning document. Don't forget, to hook this customer you are going to have to deliver a knock out presentation to sell the concept.

Later in the book I'll share some tips with you on how to build and deliver this presentation. I like to call this section *the intelligent presentation*.

Right now we have to move on to the next section of your framework agreement offer.

Chapter Summary:

- Your framework agreement must start with a covering letter or executive overview.
- It should be short but precise.
- It outlines the what, the why and the how of your proposal.
- The letter must be formal, on a company letterhead and signed by the most senior manager from your organisation.

8.

The Non-Disclosure Agreement:

Why a non disclosure agreement? Well, as we mentioned earlier providing your customer with this comprehensive framework agreement, **unsolicited**, may, in all probability lead to them issuing a RFQ or an expression of interest to your competitors. It's part of their governance policy. If you have done your homework correctly this proposal will be very attractive to them but in all probability they will have a current supplier in place! What are they going to do?

They want what you are offering, but cannot use your framework agreement (due to the non-disclosure agreement) as a tender template. As we touched on before they will find themselves between a rock and a hard place!

This is the ultimate power of a non-solicited framework proposal!

It's the Guerrilla warfare sales tactic!

If you simply approached this potential customer in pursuit of business in the normal way, and if they think your offering has merit, they may ask you to pre-qualify through their supply chain division and place you on the bidders list. But the kicker is, when you get a chance to bid you're going to have to bid against the specifications and guidelines they set! These could be based on your competitor's product or service offering as the customer doesn't know any better. This places you in a compromised position, you are trying to compete based on their rules!

When you simply offer them your framework agreement proposal, **unsolicited**, **you are changing the rules!** They have no choice other than to consider your offering based on its own merits, the way you want to propose it and this poses a problem for them as they can only compare your offer to their pre-conceived ideas and scope of their current provider's offering!

They must be able to compare Apples with Apples! But, by not allowing them to use your offer as a template, how will they be able to get a comparative quote from their current provider or any of your competition? They cannot specify any specifics of your offer, it would not be ethical! You have out manoeuvred your competition and placed yourselves in a very strong position to negotiate from a real position of strength!

Your offer is unique! No one can duplicate it!

But what is a non-disclosure/confidentiality agreement? Well I'm sure at one time or another you have all had to sign one, but for the uninitiated, this document simply states that everything pertaining to the contents, context and all inferences referred to in your framework agreement is the sole intellectual property of your organisation and cannot be disclosed, used, copied or referred to in any way, whatsoever without your explicit permission.

This means as soon as they open your document, whether they deem to sign it or not! They are legally bound by its terms and conditions under common law! The only thing they can do is decide not to look at your offer and reject your approach.

As they don't know what's in your offer without looking at it it's the perfect catch 22! Once they open it they must comply!

This sounds a bit harsh I know, but trust me, without this protection there is nothing stopping your potential customer from using your intellectual property to test the market. Once your competitors know the complexity of your offer they can easily duplicate or surpass your offer to compete.

Chapter Summary

- **It is essential** for you to include a confidentiality and non disclosure agreement within your framework offer to your customer to protect your intellectual property.
- Place the document in the 2nd section of you framework agreement after the covering letter or executive overview.
- **It must be placed before** any of your specific offer for it to have any impact or legal restraint.
- It is not essential to get the customer to sign it immediately as long as you clearly make the customer aware that you are only disclosing your offer to them under the understanding that they are aware of its existence and verbally agree to its conditions.

- **Next we shall explore what a strategic positioning statement is!**

9.

The Strategic Positioning Statement:

This statement clearly defines what your framework offer is to the customer!

It's the formal statement that defines your intentions toward the customer and discloses in broad sweeping terms what your offer consists of.

It's a strategic positioning statement, which means it positions your organisation to that of the customer's in relation to what you are offering them!

It helps you to define the scope of the agreement for the customer to understand it at a glance!

Let me give you an example:

*This positioning document serves to inform the **ACME** Group of companies the willingness of **your company** to enter into a strategic framework agreement with all of the operating business units in the **ACME** group of companies.*

*__Your company__ has identified the **ACME** group of companies as an important strategic partner for a unique and all encompassing product and service framework agreement based on **your company's xx** years experience in the specialised field of **xxx.***

This offer is based on the foundation of integrity and transparency with corporate governance at the core of our organisation culture.

*Therefore, this document is intended to inform the **ACME** Group of companies of the products and services offerings **your company** would like to extend, inclusive of the value based propositions and strategic pricing initiative, to the **ACME Group** in exchange for this preferred vendor status.*

*This strategic framework agreement is offered to the **ACME** group of companies as a first, without restriction or exclusivity for a minimum period of three (3) years.*

*It is our intention to form a specific **ACME** account management team that will be responsible to report into and liaise with a dedicated **ACME** team made up of selected operational staff, supply chain representatives and senior head office executives.*

This offer will be inclusive of, but not limited to, the products, services, responsibilities and reporting structures as identified in the accompanying scope definition of this agreement, however, the direction and executive authority will always reside within the ACME business team.

You will notice from the example that the positioning statement encompasses the comprehensive offer in a microcosm. It talks to the management and reporting functions you are offering to the customer.

In many supply contracts conducted by organisations the customer rarely has a SRM (supplier relationship management) process in place! I know it sounds crazy but it's true.

Very rarely have I come across a supply chain division that has a well defined culture of supplier relationship management. In general they place contracts with their suppliers and apart from the occasional meeting arranged by the sales organisation of their supplier, the only organisational meeting they will have is on contract renewal, when price adjustments and escalation are negotiated or when the supplier is not performing and needs a kick in the butt!

They want SRM! That's a fact, but rarely implement it? It's not that don't know how to do it; it's generally because they simply don't have the time! That's where your strategic positioning statement can place you head and shoulders above your competition! Right from the word go. You are stating up front that you have a plan. They don't have to come up with one, you've already done it!

You are in fact saying to them that you are prepared, above and beyond the role of a supply contract, to manage the relationship and take that responsibility away from them and place it squarely on your organisation shoulders. They love that! If their current supplier is not taking the initiative to do this, that's a great value add in your favour right there, before you even get your foot in the door!

In fact it's the ideal situation for you, letting your customer manage the relationship is like the tail wagging the Dog! **It may be amusing but doesn't work too good!**

Chapter Summary:

- The importance of a strategic positioning statement cannot be overstated!
- It defines your organisation's intentions in a microcosm.
- It covers the management and reporting functions that the customer rarely enjoys from the majority of their suppliers and provides them with a real compelling argument to take your offer seriously if they want a SRM process. They don't want to manage you they want you to manage for them!
- It talks to the partnering aspects of the relationship. They want that! When you talk partnering that alludes to joint responsibility for the success of the venture.
- Simply put, the strategic positioning statement tells them what they're going to get if they accept your offer. Not the details, the overview and intent!

- **Next we will focus on the scope of your framework agreement offer.**

10.

Scope Definition:

We have covered scope definition under the CRM agreement, however, in your framework agreement, this takes a different dimension!

It's not what you are contracting for, it's what you are offering to contract for. There's a big difference!

You have, I'm sure, heard the saying 'You don't get anything unless you try' or 'Nothing ventured, nothing gained'. Well this is the opportunity you have been waiting for! In a framework agreement offer you can offer your entire organisational range of equipment and services! Not just one or two products, but the lot!

Just because you have targeted this specific customer because you are aware that they have need of a particular service or product you offer, the framework agreement can encompass your whole offering.

Why not! Your targeted customer may not be aware of your entire capabilities. In fact, even if they know of you and have used your organisation in the past, you can bet your monthly salary on the fact that they have no idea of your total capabilities or what your total offering encompasses.

Here is another reason why the unsolicited framework agreement offer is your most effective Guerrilla warfare sales tactic!

In one swift move, you can outmanoeuvre more than one of your competitors at the same time. If your offer is financially attractive to the customer in one specific area of their supply chain needs, what's to say, due to your all encompassing offer, they may consider combining a number of their requirements under one roof!

If your rebate structure is attractive enough they may consider buying your entire range because when viewed as a whole they can combine a considerable amount of their requirements and responsibility under one roof and reap better rewards and economy of scale from one supplier!

Any one product or service you offer, viewed on its own merits, may be more expensive than your competitors, however when viewed as a package deal, they become attractive because of the economies of scale and the one-stop-shop effect!

So, don't be afraid to offer every aspect of your organisations capabilities. They may not want it all, but confuse them anyway, who knows? Maybe you'll get lucky!

Please remember the scope definition is not the products and services definition! It's the overall definition of what scope of works and management abilities you are capable of and prepared to take responsibility for contractually.

Chapter Summary:

- Your scope definition is the statement you make in your framework agreement offer that defines the total capabilities and responsibilities you are prepared to contract for.
- Don't be afraid to encompass all of your organisational capabilities. The customer may have other suppliers undertaking these activities at present, however, given your offer they may consider taking advantage of the economies of scale your offer provides for!
- Remember some of your service or product offering may, when viewed alone, be more expensive than your competition, but offered as a package deal may make a lot of financial sense to your customer!
- Remember, 'Nothing ventured, nothing gained!"

- **Next we can define the product and service offering**

11.

Products and Services' Definition:

In this section you get to list and define, in detail, all of your products and related services you are offering under the agreement.

Broad definitions and descriptions are the order of the day here, with references to part No's and specifications that can be found under separate cover or added to the back of your framework agreement offer as part of an annexure.

Do not be tempted to add 6000 products here! Something in the back of your customers head will explode!!

Descriptions of products categories are sufficient!

As mentioned under the scope definition section, don't be afraid to encompass your entire range of capabilities, but a word of warning! Only offer what you can really manage and excel at!

Chapter Summary:

- Your product and service definition is a detailed list of all of your organisations capabilities, product and services you want to offer the customer.
- This is your opportunity to offer all of your capabilities regardless of whether the customer wants them or not.
- Do not go into part number detail but rather list product categories and service definitions. Refer to annexure information for the finer detail or supply additional documentation to back up your offer.
- Make this list as comprehensive as possible; remember the economies of scale that you could be offering the customer. Don't be shy; go for it!

- **In the next section of your framework agreement offer you must detail how you will manage this account for the customer. I prefer to describe it as how you will project manage the account, who will be involved, and how will your team will report and interface into the customers team.**

12.

The Account Management Team:

This section of the agreement focuses on the people aspect of your offer. Who will manage this account from you team and who else will be involved, what their roles and responsibilities will be and how these processes will add value to the customer's account.

It would be advisable to refer to the names, age and experience of all of these resources. The specific roles they will perform and their responsibilities to the customer account. In addition you can refer to their C.V's in finer detail in the annexure of your offer or under separate cover if you think it's applicable.

Once you have detailed their reporting structures and responsibilities it really helps to show these relationships by way of an organogram clearly defining the structure and who reports to whom!

Let me give you an example of 2 graphics, depicting one of my client's framework agreements with a mining house who has 87 operating mining sites!

The Acme Group Account Management Team:

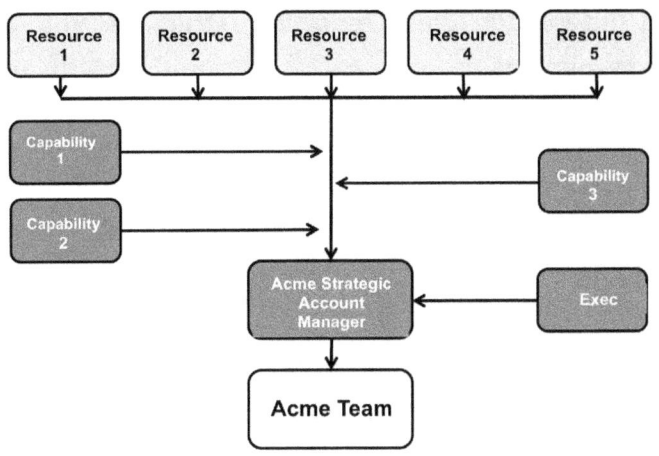

Reporting Methodology

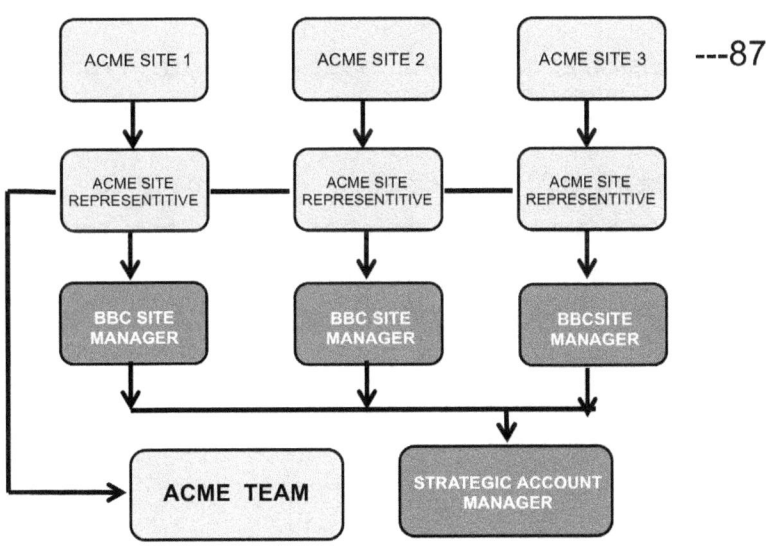

---87

Both of these organogram are simple, but a graphic is worth a thousand words when you're trying to explain the interaction and reporting structure you are recommending.

In the above graphic the important element to point out is the dual reporting lines at the ACME head office level. You'll note that for governance and to act as an integrity check on information received, the ACME HQ team will receive operational reports from both their site team representatives and the supplier's strategic account manager. This ensures accuracy and transparency of the information.

We must constantly keep the customer in the loop;

The customer always wants to feel they are in control, so this kind of reporting structure is recommended.

In regard to the resources you commit to your customer, back office activities like logistics, costing, scheduling and accounting activities, there is no harm in telling the customer that you will commit a dedicated team to their account for these activities when these people , in fact, are shared resources within your business.

The essential thing is committing certain individuals within these departments to liaise with the customer on their account. **The same people every time!** Remember you are attempting to build a rock solid relationship with this customer!

When it comes to the face-to-face resources, the account manager and the project manager, these also need to be dedicated to this account. **Don't change people or the customer may change you!**

However these individuals may be used to manage the accounts of multiple customers as long as they are in the same industry. In my team, one of my guys was the account manager for the Hydrocarbon processing industries. In short he managed all of the oil Refineries in our region! Because of the CRM processes in place with each customer he and his team were able to handle three major accounts at once!

They had their strategic operational meetings with a different customer each week. The reason you have to have a team focus on a specific industry is to build their expertise in that discipline, they get better and better in managing these customers as their experience grows!

This is how you calibrate your organisation and your solutions for success! If you develop a value based solution for one of these customers you can pitch your proposition to the other two customers with high levels of confidence that they will buy it!

If you don't commit a team to this process you are not differentiating your organisation from any of the others the customer is dealing with!

In addition to the operational team that will be dedicated to managing this customer account, don't overlook the importance of your executive team in this picture! You should always try to show an internal reporting function of the account manager direct to the executive board. In fact it's a good idea to commit one of your executives as a sponsor for this venture to add legitimacy and additional customer confidence in your offer.

Chapter Summary:

- The documenting of your committed account management team is an essential part of your framework agreement offer.
- Back office and company resources can be shared but a committed team from these departments needs to be assigned to interact with your account customer. You need to identify them up front and not change them if possible
- The account manager and other important account functions, based on the size of the customer account, should be dedicated as much as possible.
- Remember to detail each team member's role, activities and reporting structures in addition to their individual or teams' responsibilities in the running of the account.
- Use an organogram and flow charts to graphical explain these reporting structures.
- Remember to show your organisation executive's role in the management of this account. You must always show an executive overview internal reporting line to the account manager. This gives the customer assurances

that they have the support of your executive board in the management of their account.

- It's not a bad idea to commit an executive sponsor from your organisation to oversee this account. This will provide the customer with an additional level of confidence.

- **The next section of you framework agreement is the performance criteria. How will you benchmark the performance of the account management team?**

13.

Performance Criteria

How will you measure the effectiveness and efficiencies of your account management team? In this section of your framework offer you are going to have to explain that to the customer!

It's easier than you think! How would you conduct the management process of handing this kind of account on a day-to-day basis in your organisation? You must have policies and procedures your people follow and work to, right? You need to document the average monthly activities your account management team will perform to manage this account!

What will be the duties of the account manager? When will he or she do this and that? By what date will he or she report to the customer on the financial results in any month? What will be the report structure and what will it contain? How long is it proposed to take to report on quarterly results and how will he or she presents the walk forward forecasts for expenditure and revenue streams to the customer?

For every discipline or job roll you are offering your customer in the agreement you must document their deadlines and monthly activities on behalf of the customer. **The more complex it looks the more value for their money the customer perceives!**

I'll give you an example, in the account management team section, I gave you an organogram of how one of my clients interface into their customer team. Two examples of the performance criteria for this team are as follows:

Performance Criteria

Group Site managers

- First point of contact on site with site specific ACME resources

- Regular site visits by or before the 15th of each Month.

- Inspection of ---------
- verification to-----------------------
- Identification of ----------------------------

- Recommendations regarding-------------
- Reporting all of the above into the account manager, management accountant and administrative team via the standard report as detailed in annexure 1.

- Close working relationship with the **BBC Company** logistic planners.
- Constant contact with the Strategic Account Manager.
- The eyes and ears of the Strategic Account Manager on site.

Strategic Account Manager

The Strategic Account Manager would be a dynamic person responsible for co-ordinating the entire project. The Strategic Account Manager will be accountable for the following competencies:

- First line of contact into the ACME Group, nationally

- Responsible for all facets of the offered scope

- Full accountability to the designated ACME Team

- Responsible for aligning the joint teams' strategy objectives

- Responsible for all site teams and **BBC companies** resource deployment

- Providing current and future product and service 'road maps' to the ACME Team

- Reporting monthly on all activities and tactical plan implementations for each region and each BU
- Reporting monthly on all financial results obtained by site activities

- Presenting future plans encompassing 3, 6, 9 and 12 month forecasts

- Understanding the financial impact of decisions on both **BBC Company** and the **ACME Group**

- Consultative problem solving
- Orchestrating and management of company resources

- Establishing a vision of a committed customer/ supplier relationship

- Engaging ACME on the creation of SVO's (Shared Value Outcomes)

- Identifying the critical elements of the **ACME** Group's working methodologies where true value can be applied

- Working closely with the **ACME** team to identify and develop joint strategies to increase the value based relationship

- Ensuring that all Health and Safety standards as prescribed by the act and the **ACME** Group are adhered to.

- It is envisaged that each **BBC Company** Site manager will visit an **ACME** site on or before the 15th of each month. They, together with the **ACME** site representative will complete the standard report as detailed in Annexure 1 and forward this report to the account manager no later than the 20th of the month.

- The account manager will in turn correlate this data into the combined regional report as detailed in annexure 1A for presentation to the **ACME HQ** team on the 25th of each calendar Month.

- **It will be the strategic account manager's responsibility to present this information, value roadmaps, time scales, recommendations and expected value release on a 3, 6, 9 and 12 month forecast flash and walk forward report.**

Ok, so if you document each player's role, in addition to their reporting deadlines, the customer has an in-depth view of your organisations professionalism and capabilities in handling their account.

Chapter Summary:

- It is essential that you define the roles, working methodologies and responsibilities of your account management team.
- When you define who will do what, how they will do it and when it will get done, the customer can get an in depth view of your organisations capabilities!
- List all divisional roles and important individuals' responsibilities within those divisions in relation to the overall management of the customer's account.
- It's about you being able to document your organisational capabilities and performance levels to show you are able to guarantee sustainable levels of high performance and repeatable results.

- **The next section of your agreement offer is the Customer relationship management plan.**

14.

The Customer Relationship Management Plan (CRM):

We have covered, in detail, what a generic CRM plan entails earlier in this body of work, so we don't have to duplicate it here. The important thing in this section of your framework offer is to allude to the fact that should the customer want to take you up on this comprehensive offer, that in Phase I of the implementation plan, a strategic meeting will be held where an 'Alignment' process will need to take place. This is your CRM plan!

At this meeting, certain areas of the account management process will need to be discussed, agreed upon and documented. This is the time you sit with the customer and complete the CRM planning document we discussed earlier. This will cement the organisation working methodology between the two organisations and act as **'The Glue between the Two'**

In your framework agreement offer you can document this process in a separate section on its own or you can simply detail the process under the implementation plan section. Whereever you decide to put it, just remember to list the CRM process headings for discussion **this is an essential element to show the customer you have a plan!**

The discussion topics are listed under the CRM Chapter Summary on page 83.

15.

The Implementation Plan

In any undertaking, such as a comprehensive framework agreement, it would be surprising to be able to jump straight in and implement the whole project immediately. It does depend on the type of agreement you are tabling, but in general, there's a lot of work to do before you can start.

The customer knows this and if they are going to give you a chance to prove yourselves, they probably would feel a phased-in approach would be the best approach. So give them one!

Give the customer a phased implementation plan! In the previous chapter we talked of the alignment process or, as we know it, the CRM plan. You are going to have to conduct this kick-off meeting with the customer as soon as possible to agree on the ground rules and working methodology, so that's got to happen in phase I. What other activities will happen in phase I? What do you want to achieve in phase II and III?

With your team, you need to give this section of your framework agreement a lot of consideration! You do not want to scare the customer off trying to do everything at once but on the other hand you don't want to take 6 months before you start making any money out of this account, so what makes sense?

Some of the more obvious phases of this type of agreement we touched on earlier in the book. If you are going to use phased-in pricing as an incentive for the customer then this will only be applicable in year one of the contract so it must form part of your phase I implementation plan. In year 2 you will introduce the rebate structure base on the received volumes of work, now that's a logical phased implementation plan! However, there are financial phases and logistical phases, so be careful not to mix these two up. Keep the financial implementation plan in your strategic offer section or even in the value based proposition section of your offer. This section is strictly for the logistical roll out plan of your framework offer!

Proposing 23 Phases in a project implementation may raise some eyebrows with the Customer but 2 to 4 phases is sufficient to convince the customer you are being careful, while still demonstrating you know what you're doing!

It's quite amazing but in recent months, I have been present at a number of my client's customer presentations offering these framework agreements where after the presentation the customer's have stated if they get the go ahead to accept this offer, they want to move to Phase III or IV immediately! Go figure! It appears that they were so impressed with the detail and comprehensive nature of my client's offer that they wanted to skip any intermediate steps and go straight for the full implementation! That's the power of the intelligent presentation. It can really convince the customer to commit. More on this later!

So, a phased implementation plan can work to your benefit in a number of ways. it doesn't scare the customer away, It can convince the customer you know what you're doing, it gives you time to plan and put resources into place and it stops you biting off more than you can chew on a complex account.

Once you deliver your framework offer presentation, don't be surprised if the customer comes up with their own priorities that supersede yours!

Once they see your implementation plan it can kick in a whole series of initiatives on the part of the customer team as you have provided them with a reason to rethink their whole approach to this supply chain requirement. This often happens so don't be defensive or protective of your implementation plan. Go with the flow as it may result in a whole new ball game.

Again, the power of the open framework agreement offer is that it is the guerilla warfare sales pre-emptive strike! The customer can't protect themselves against it; they can only deal with the aftermath! It's a fascinating strategy!

Chapter Summary:

- A' Phased' in Implementation plan is a safe way to embark on a framework agreement plan.
- Think about a using a 2 to 4 phase approach to roll out your plan so as not to scare the customer with too many changes at once!
- You can't do too much before you have your CRM strategy meeting anyway, so you already need a phase I step to think about the logical roll out sequences for phases II & III
- Provide the customer as much detail in this roll out plan as possible, don't be vague. If they think you haven't put enough thought into this essential part of your framework offer, you may blow the deal!
- It is a good idea to attach some shared value outcomes (SVO's) to the completion of these phases, or, at least some recognisable financial milestones. The customer will want to see this and it will all add to the attractiveness of your offer!
- Don't mix your financial incentives up with your implementation phases. Keep them separate. The financial offer is section 15 of your framework offer.

- The next section of your offer needs to document your strategic offer.

16.

The strategic Offer

In this section of your framework offer, you need to list all of the immediate financial benefits you are offering the customer, should they agree to enter into an agreement with you.

This strategic offer is based solely on the customer agreeing to enter into a 3 year, non-exclusive agreement. So, you have nothing to fear.

Before embarking on this framework agreement initiative your target customer must represent a considerable amount of work for you to consider them for this special treatment in the first place. Therefore you should be aware of the kind of volumes of work you could secure if you are successful. You must base your strategic offer on these expected volumes.

In chapter 5 we describe some of the ways we can make our strategic offers attractive. Some of these initiatives include our first year phased in pricing, rebate structures and so on, but at the heart of our offer we must always consider our other partners in this business: our principles suppliers!

We must not forget what these additional volumes can mean to them! If we manufacture in house we need to approach our raw material suppliers before we make our framework offer to ascertain what additional discounts we could receive from them if we secured this extra work and they benefit from larger volume orders from us! When it comes to our principals, what would these forecasted volumes mean to them? Could we secure additional volume discounts from them if we placed quarterly scheduled bulk orders on the factory? We must explore every avenue to make our strategic offer as attractive as possible, as we have said before you are only going to get one shot at this, so make sure it's your best!

Chapter Summary:

- Your strategic offer must be bulleted, simple but as extensive and multilayered as possible.
- Be careful you don't offer volume discounts or rebates that can be misconstrued by the customer as being cumulative. That means for every volume milestone they reach they cannot add the last volume discount to the new one offered for the next tier. Each tier has its own specific rebate structure!

- **Your next challenge is to construct your value based Proposition where you add all these incentives up and add them to your value added contributions to the customer's business.**

17.

The Value Based Proposition

This is where we started at the beginning of this book! What is a value based proposition? Well, we have come pretty far down the road and the penultimate part of your framework agreement offer is to spell out for the customer what this entire body of work and detailed comprehensive offer results in for them! The bottom line: **what's in it for them?**

Why do we have to spell it out for them? Well, if you know anything about supply chain processes the entire division, both on customer sites and at head office level is tasked year on year to secure new and innovative ways to reduce or at the worst case limit the cost of doing business with their suppliers, their bonus and yearly increase depends on it!

This means they are continuously looking to secure additional savings from their suppliers! As stated previously, when a supplier has a contract that's about it. There's very little the supply chain can do to squeeze additional savings from them. That's why when we upset the applecart with our unsolicited approach, if it makes sense, they will jump at the chance!

If we can summarise a considerable potential saving year on year over and above their current status quo, it's very hard for them to resist! **But don't expect them to do the math!**

You have to spell it out for them!

So what should your value based proposition look like? Well the first part should be the total commercial incentives derived from your initial discount structures, phased-in pricing savings and any rebates based on a projected volume of business for one year.

Added to this, you need to total up the projected savings you can provide them by saving them on things like labour costs, (MTTR) and (MTBF) figures you have calculated (as discussed previously) in fact any projected value added savings your framework agreement will provide for them!

When you total this lot up you may be surprised! It will come to a lot of money in one year. Now you project the total savings they can expect over the total 3 years agreement. This will be substantial.

Do not, I repeat do not express this as an overall percentage! This would be a critical error. Simply express it in real money! It will have a greater effect on

the customer at a personal level! Percentages mean nothing when you're dealing with them all Day but real money, that's different!

So, there you have it, apart from the customer agreement your framework agreement offer is almost complete! How big should it be? Well based on over twenty I have constructed for my clients over the last few years between 50 and 80 pages! That's a substantial document!

But you are only half way there yet! You still have to sell this concept to the customer! You are going to have to build a knock out presentation to position this initiative with the customer! This will take you just as long to build and prepare for as the original agreement!

Chapter Summary

- Your value based proposition is, in many ways, the most important part of your agreement's offer!
- If it's not attractive enough, you could have wasted a lot of your precious time!
- Remember to first total up the financial incentives you are offering the customer via your discount structures based on an expected yearly volume.
- Then total up all of the additional value added savings your offer provides the customer in one year.
- Add both of these savings together and project them over the 3 year agreement.
- Express this total contract saving in real monetary terms! Do not use percentages!

- **The last section of your offer should be a Heads of Agreement the customer can sign!**

18.

Heads of Agreement

Including a Heads of agreement in the back of your unsolicited framework offer may seem, to many, to be the epitome of cheek, but to others it shows extreme confidence! The point is, whenever you enter into a contract with any organisation there comes a point where the two parties have to negotiate the commercial terms and conditions! The sales organisation bases their proposal on their standard terms and conditions, and the customer bases their contract on theirs! This is generally a stalemate situation.

I suggest you supersede this stumbling block by submitting a heads of agreement that combines both sets of T & C's with any suggested modifications you would like to suggest! In fact get a copy of the customers T & C's and read them. In most cases a simple statement in the heads of agreement to the fact that this agreement is subject to the customer's standard terms and conditions with the following negotiable changes, is sufficient to put the argument to bed. Pre-empt the situation.

Do not give the customer any reason to hesitate over your offer.

This heads of agreement document is the simplest you have to create as it simply states that the agreement is based on your submitted framework agreement offer. No detail is required; you have 60 pages of detail before the heads of agreement. A signature and date from both parties is all you need!

In most cases the customer will never sign this agreement! They will eventually give you one of theirs to sign. So why bother in the first place? Gamesmanship is the answer! You want them to know you want this work and you are extremely confident that they will want what you are offering. They will want you to commit to your offer! What better sign of commitment can you show than providing them with a heads of agreement to sign!

So, there you have it! If you follow these guidelines you now have a framework agreement offer to submit to your customer but remember, you haven't finished yet, there's still the matter of the presentation you will need to deliver to win this deal.

That's next!

Chapter Summary:

- Your Heads of agreement is a sign of extreme confidence and the willingness to commit to your promises!
- Include, at the back of your Heads of agreement the T&C's you are willing to accept, or a statement to the fact that the agreement is based on the customers T&C's with the following negotiated changes.
- No other details are required. The start date for the contract has already been stipulated in your Implementation and phasing proposal and all other contractual details are as per your framework agreement.

- **The next challenge is to build your Intelligent Presentation!**

19.

The Presentation Plan

Ok, you now have a framework agreement offer to present to your customer, the emphasis being on present! To pull this off you are going to have to give them a closing presentation designed to win you this deal. Why a closing presentation? Well that is what your presentation has to be designed to do. Close the deal! Earlier, in the account pursuit strategy plan we finished off at the presentation plan. Here is the detailed plan I promised you!

There are many kinds of presentations we deliver to our customers, some are designed to inform, some to educate and some to sell, but for the life of me, I am beginning to think this fact is lost on most of the sales organisations I deal with! All of their customer presentations seem to blend in. They are all too technical, too long and terribly boring! In short 'Death by PowerPoint' I talked around this subject at the beginning of this book. If you want to convince your customer to award you a deal you had better design a bespoke presentation designed to do just that! No more, no less!

This is especially important when you are presenting to win a framework agreement. This is not your normal pitch for business. If you secure this work it may represent $20, $30 or $100 million dollars of business to your organisation a year! This is the big league Dude! You better bring your best game as you will only get one shot at this big prize!

Bespoke is the key word here! If you were to go to all this trouble and effort to build a comprehensive framework agreement offer to your customer and then deliver your generic presentation regarding your companies basic history and capabilities what has that presentation got to do with this deal?

Bespoke people, bespoke. The customer has to be convinced by this presentation that your framework agreement is special. It's just for them! It is unique!

What is the one simple way we can achieve this?

Brand your presentation, that's how! Your customer has spent millions creating their branding in the market place; the least we can do is use it in your presentation to them! Branding and subliminal techniques are sure fire ways of turning both your framework agreement and your presentation to them into unique bespoke submissions.

Subliminal techniques! Aren't they illegal? Well yes. They are if you put them in a movie! But the subliminal techniques I'm referring to is to customise your agreement document and your presentation with as many visual cues as possible to demonstrate to the customer that you know their business.

Insert pictures of their manufacturing sites, their Head office, pictures from their website. Any subliminal message you can, to convince them, subtly, that your organisation knows their business, their market place and their challenges.

A few years ago this would have been very difficult and costly but not now, all this takes is some thought, some time, the Internet and your cell phone camera!

What other strategies can we adopt to make our framework agreement presentation bespoke and convincing to the customer? Let's look at a comprehensive intelligent presentation plan to truly appreciate the effort we have to put into building a presentation to win!

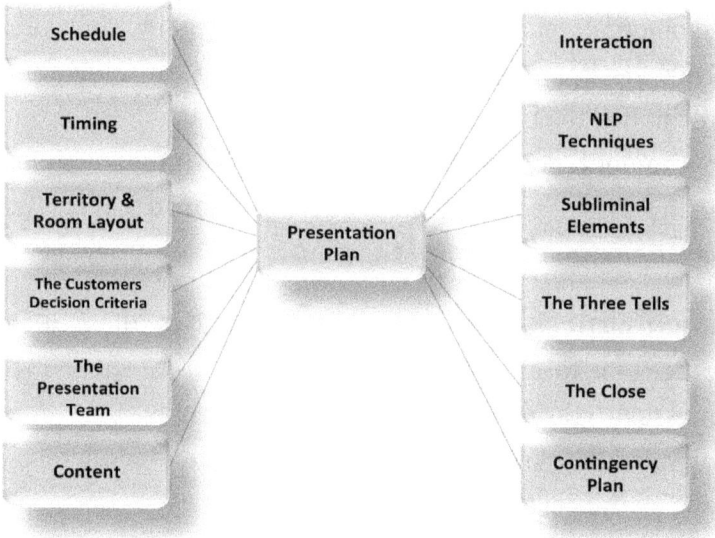

This is a presentation strategy plan encompassing all the elements of an intelligent presentation designed to win!

Let's take each element in turn and build our bespoke framework agreement presentation together!

The Schedule

What do we have to plan for? Quite a lot as it happens. We not only have to plan when we will present this deal to the customer but the whole sequence of events leading up to that point. If we don't, we will run out of time and have to take short cuts, we don't want that with something as important as this presentation.

Let me give you the full run down required:

Firstly, to build a winning presentation at this level will take you approximately 20 minutes preparation time for every 1 minute you intend to present. Let me spell that out for you! Generally a customer will give you 35 to 45 minutes to present your case, they have learnt the hard way (Death by PowerPoint!) So, given that as a guideline, if you are going to present for 40 minutes it's going to take you at least **13 Hours preparation time!**

Another rule of thumb I have gained by 40 years experience at this game is that to build a winning presentation is that each slide you present should take between 3 and 5 minutes to present! Why? Because, if you build your slides correctly you are going to enlist customer interaction on every point you present and they are going to want to ask you stuff!!

So, how many slides are you now going to try to present? This is the singular, most common error made by sales people! They try to present **60 slides** in 40 minutes! **You think!!** It's impossible, never going to happen, never!

If you have 40 minutes to present do not plan on presenting more than 12 slides tops! What!!!! I hear you cry! We could never do that! We could never get our story across with so few slides. It's impossible!

Well in here lies the crunch! You can and you must! Remember you have a 60 paged document you can refer to, you don't have to go into detail, you simply have to present the **value based proposal!** You can do that in 12 slides, trust me; I have done it successfully for 30 years!

So, what's going to take you 13 Hours? Let's look at what you need to do!

- You need to set the date for this presentation to the customer. (Don't worry about the logistics and customers yet. That's still to come)

- You need to build the presentation. (Don't worry about the content yet)

- You need to do one dry run to check on the content and the timing.

- You need to do another dry run to check on the delivery style and planned customer interaction dynamics with your team.

- You need to run another dry run to check on the validity and timing of your trial close and final closing technique.

- Finally, you have to do the dress rehearsal with your full team with executive feedback to finely tune your delivery.

Still think 13 Hours is too long?

If I'm any judge, which I am, if you're not careful you will spend so much time building the presentation you won't have time to do any dry runs, and that my friends turns your presentation from a great one to a mediocre one!

If you end up reading your slides and looking at your own presentation instead of engaging with the customer or if you ask a question to the room, rather than direct it to one of your customers by name, or worse, refer to the customer as 'you people' or 'you guys', you could seriously jeopardise your chances of winning this deal.

Gary Player, the South African Golfer is famous for saying

"The more I practice it seems, the luckier I get"

You should know the contents of your presentation like the back of your hand, any referral to pieces of paper or having to read your slides will tell the customer you don't really know this material and it won't come across as compelling! If you don't know this material have you done this kind of deal before? Do you really know what you're doing? Do you sound convinced in what you are proposing?

The intelligent presenter uses the bullets on their slides to simply remind them of what they need to talk about next! They know the material but they haven't tried to remember it word for word, like a Shakespearian actor because they aren't one! If you attempt to learn a presentation word for word you will get into a world of trouble in a New York minute and we know how long that is right!

Dry runs with your team are the only way I know to get this right! Remember you only have one shot at this!

So, in summary, when embarking on the initiative of a framework agreement offer, make allowances for sufficient time to build the winning presentation. You cannot practice too much!

Timing

You would be forgiven for thinking this is the same as planning your schedule, but it's not! Timing is one of the most essential elements to consider when planning a winning presentation!

Timing is everything!

Firstly when would you prefer to present to your customer? What Day? Does it matter? What about what time of Day you present, does that matter? Well if you believe the statistics research organisations continually circulate, yes it does, it matters a lot!

To present on a Monday or a Friday may not be the brightest thing you could do! I think that's pretty obvious! I'm old enough to remember that back in the dark ages you wouldn't want to buy a car that was assembled in the factory on either a Monday or a Friday. That might be a costly mistake! It's the same here. Your customer will not thank you for putting them in a serious think mode on either of these days, they have different priorities on their mind.

The experts say Tuesday to Thursday is the best time; the customer is in work mode and thinking clearly. The same goes for the time of day. The experts say presenting in the morning is better than the afternoon - especially at 3:30 PM In the afternoon!

But do you have a choice?

I know a lot of you reading this will be thinking we have no choice, the customer dictates when we can present to them right! Well not really, especially in this case. As you are contacting them unsolicited, you would be forgiven for thinking you are in an even weaker position than normal, but you are not!

You are offering them a chance to reposition their supplier status quo! The offer of a framework agreement is a little different to their normal routine. They may be convinced by a strong argument that this opportunity is so important, their senior management or executive must attend, so can we set a future date for this presentation at such and such a time when they are available? Sounds reasonable to me! You may well be able to choose your battle and even the battlefield for this contest! (Remember Sun Tzu.)

As a last resort, if they give you a slot to present that you are unhappy with, simply tell them you can't make that date and provide them with alternative day and time. You'll never get anything unless you try!

On a slightly different tack, that may or may not be applicable to presenting a framework agreement offer, if you are presenting in a competitive scenario, timing is also extremely important! When do you want to present first or last?

I am always fascinated when I ask my clients this question; the answers are varied but consistently in the favour of going first! The reasoning behind this seems to be if you really give a great presentation this will set the bar for anyone following you and the first presentation will always stick in the customer's mind!

To a point, I can't really take issue with any of this reasoning, however, my reasoning has always been squarely rooted in the belief that exposing your intellectual property to the customer when they still have other competitors to see is extremely dangerous!

I am not proposing that the customer will intentionally reveal the innermost details of you proposal to your competitor to enable them to compare apples with apples! **They wouldn't do that would they!**

I'm just concerned that, as the customer is not the expert in your field of expertise, that these confidential elements of your proposal may be leaked to your competition in the form of comparison seeking questions! Your competitor is not a fool! Where is the customer coming up with these detailed product or capability related questions? They must stem from someone else's proposal! **This is not Rocket science!**

My view is always, always go last! If nothing else, if you try to close the deal at the presentation, as you should, there is a possibility they may shake your hand if you go last. This will never happen if you go first or second!

Finally on the point of timing, it would be very advantageous to pitch your framework agreement at the right time of year! If you are dealing with listed companies the end of every quarter is not such a good time to pitch as the organisation is preparing their interim results for their shareholders! No big changes will happen for at least one month either side of this time! Again the 3rd quarter of the year may be a very good time to pitch this offer as the supply chain may seriously need some additional saving to make their targets! It's also budget planning time! You'll never have a better opportunity!

I'll leave you to consider these strategies on their own merits!

Territory and Room Layout

Your territory or theirs? That's a good question! What do you think? In most cases this question would not come up and I think this is a great shame!

The opportunity to ask the customer if you could host them for this important presentation is a fantastic tactic, as, based on how you position it, and if they decide to take you up on this offer, it can indicate the levels of interest they have in your company!

You're positioning!

This is especially true if you invite senior management from their side to attend and they accept! What does this tell you?

I think they're interested, don't you?

There are other very important aspects and tactics to this strategy that don't immediately spring to mind! Can you think of any?

Let's list some!

- You are in your comfort zone and they aren't.

- They have to spend time and money to come to you; they are going to want to leverage this opportunity!

- You are proposing, to the customer, that you have all of the resources and capabilities to provide them with a fantastic framework offer! If they come to you, you can give them a tour of your facilities. You can prove it to them!

- You can dictate the timing and pace of the presentation!

- In regards to the room layout you can place name tags at the table to split the customer up. You don't want an 'us and them' or a confrontational seating arrangement. You also want to be able to address them by name!

- You can arrange a U shaped table to facilitate maximum customer interaction and view of your presentation.
- You can make sure your equipment is working and your Data projector does not get in the way. (Ceiling mount is best)

- It is much easier to cater for a contingency plan if you are presenting at your own facility!

- You can bring multiple experts into the presentation to cover specialised areas of your presentation! (They don't have to be at the table continuously)

- All of your materials and resources are at hand if you need them!

- **You don't have any of these luxuries if you have to go to them!**

But, what if you have to go to them to present your offer? What can you do to tip the odds of success in your favour?

Here are some tips!

- On setting up the presentation ask who you can liaise with regarding the presentation room.

- Contact this person with the intent of visiting the facilities to check them out before you present.

- Ask if it's possible to have a U shaped table arrangement?

- Check the equipment works with your laptops!

- Ask if it's possible to arrive and set up at least one hour before you are scheduled to present?

- Make name tags to take with you!

- Ask if there is an adjacent room some of your people can use, just in case you need them. (Remember don't overpower the customer with too many people at the table!)

That's it, that's all I have regarding territory and your room layout strategy. These strategies aren't easy to accomplish, and they take a lot of time and effort. That's why they represent such success factors and differentiators when you do succeed in pulling them off!

The Customer Decision Criteria

What better strategy could you come up with than to know, in advance, what your customers decision criteria will be, before you present a solution to them!

If you can give them everything they want, how can they possibly say No!

Well, that's what I want you to be able to do!

How can you secure this information?

It's actually easier than you think! You simply have to ask the right person!

When initially setting up this framework presentation you are going to have to deal with the supply chain head at the customers Head office. (As mentioned previously)

At the same time as you make the offer of this unsolicited presentation, it's the perfect time to set an exploratory meet and greet session with this person. Don't tell them you want to discuss decision criteria with them, just secure the meeting to introduce yourself. You can touch on the decision criteria when you are with them. You simply have to ask them if there are any specific areas they want you to focus on when you present.

They won't be able to stop themselves! As tower head they do not want you to waste their time or that of their direct reports! This would embarrass them, so beware, remember to take a pad and pencil with you; you're going to need it!

If you approach the subject in the right way they will dictate a lot of the parameters you will have to cover when you present. Nothing could be easier! It's the supply chain tower head who is responsible for introducing new initiatives to the supply chain; they normally do not let an opportunity like this slip through their fingers! Again for them, it's nothing ventured, nothing gained.

They may tell you that they have selected vendors in the specific area you are focusing on and they cannot promise you anything. In fact they may try to talk you out of it, but stick to your guns, they don't know what you're going to offer them yet! It is essential that you secure the opportunity to present! **That's the critical objective!**

Now, once you have these basic decision criteria, you would be pretty silly not to build those elements into your framework agreement under the headings I have given you.

In the account pursuit section of the book, remember we make mention of the Technical client review process the TCR! This is where the sales team picks up a great deal of information regarding the customers decision criteria, that's why, under normal competitive bidding situations it can be such a game changing tactic!

Whatever way you obtain this information, pay special attention to focus on these criteria in your presentation to the customer. This is very important information; as it shows the tower head you have taken their advice, protect his or her position and serves to prove to the customer you know their business and have catered for their needs.

In instances where you know the customer, this process is even simpler! If you know who you will be presenting to, phone each one of them after the date for the presentation is set, and ask them as they will be attending the presentation, what special areas they would like you to focus on!

They will all have different agendas and interest areas so what better opportunity would you want than to focus on each individual during the presentation and address each of the needs in turn!

Quite frankly, I don't know any other way to present a value based solution to a customer! If you don't know their decision criteria your simply pitching in the dark aren't' you?

Ok, that's all I have to say regarding the customer's decision criteria. Let's move to your presentation team.

The Presentation Team

Do you need a presentation team? Yes you do! Imagine, if you sent one person to present at this level, what would the customer think? Imagine if they asked some difficult questions and he or she was unable to answer them?

You need a team to back each other up and establish the legitimacy of your offer. The higher up the management chain your team is, the better your case will appear! Your senior management don't have to present, they just have to be there!

As a general rule, for every specific specialised discipline represented within your framework offer, (with the exception of your accounts people) need to be represented on your presentation team! Not necessarily at the table, but available should you need them!

That's why you need to secure a caucus room for the additional members of your team to wait until they are needed. Don't bring them and have them wait in some corridor outside the presentation room or worse, sit at the back of the room while the presentation is being delivered. Why! Well they will interrupt and jump in to the presentation if their area of speciality is being discussed, even if you don't need their help. It's only natural, they will want to participate but it may destroy the flow of your presentation!

Your core presentation team should not exceed 3 or 4 people. Any more will be viewed by the customer as heavy handed.

Who will be your main presenter, well, not the incumbent account manager, that's for sure! Not unless he or she has had extensive sales experience and presentation exposure! Remember your account manager types are your farmers they are not your hunters!

Your presenter has to be the best presenter you have. I don't care what division they work for, you need them for this one task. Win this job! Your head presenter has to be the consummate professional; any less would be to pay lip service to this opportunity!

It is essential that the core team presenting your proposal work together to build the strategy for the presentation. Be careful, the senior executive who will be attending the presentation may think they do not need to attend the strategy meeting or any of the dry runs! **This will be a serious mistake!**

If they are not fully briefed on your strategy they will also jump in during your presentation uninvited and could even contradict you as they don't fully appreciate the context of what's being discussed!

I'm sure this has happened to you at some time or another; I know it's happened to me, it's as though they truly believe they can simply pitch up, without any insight into the strategy and contribute! Bless them!

Your presentation team must work like a formula 1 pit crew, everyone knows their job, the part they will play in the presentation and they complement each other members' contribution.

Finally, let's talk about the dress code! I know this is a sticky subject to day but trust me it's still very important. When you are presenting this level of presentation, at your customers head office you have to look the part! I don't care whether you wild cat oil baron, jeans won't cut it here! Business suits people!

When coaching my clients on this level of presentation, I even insist on the old standby of the dark blue or black business suit, no flashy stuff! You're not in the music business! (If you are, I apologise!)

For the women in our teams, try not to wear floral pattern dresses, they are very pretty and that's the problem they can detract away from what you are saying to what you're wearing! It's a fact! Business suits are called for here!

I don't have to tell you the oldest saying in business 'You can always dress down but you can't dress up'

Right, that about cover's it for your presentation team, let's move on the nitty-gritty stuff, the content of your presentation.

Content

You have 12 slides what are you going to put on them? Well in fact you have 13 because the very first slide is your launch slide! This slide is the first thing the customer see's. It has to immediately tell the customer what your presentation is about. It must have visual impact and contain the subliminal elements we have touched on previously. Let me show you an example of a launch slide to give you an idea of what I mean.

This slide incorporates both company logos (made up) and a subliminal message depicting a group of business men shaking hands. The obvious inference is they are making a deal! The slide also introduces the topic of the presentation and the organisations branding. The next slide in your presentation should be an overview of what the presentation is about.

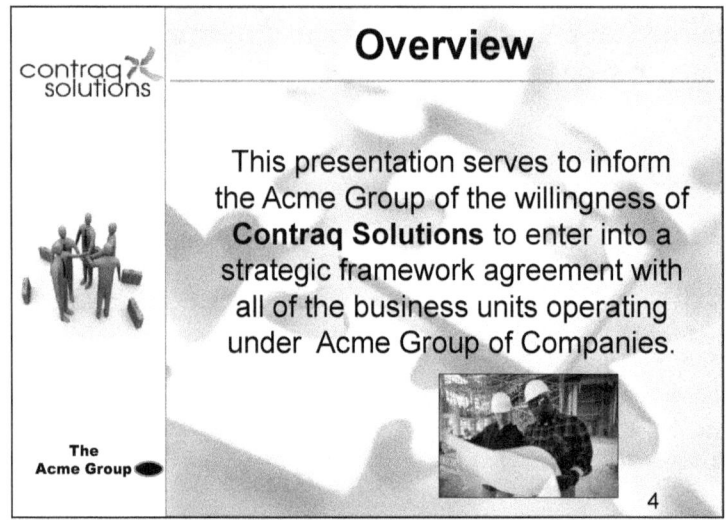

Simple and straight to the point! This slide defines your intent and the reason for the presentation. Ok, 11 Sides to go, what's next?

You are now going to introduce your customer to the topics and content of your presentation. This slide is very important for three reasons. Firstly you want to enlist agreement from the customer that your presentation has merit and that they are happy with what you are about to show them. Secondly, a content slide allows you to establish a structure the customer can follow and thirdly, the slide forms the first part of your three tells structure. (More on this later)

In addition to those elements a content slide allows you to establish agreement from the customer that the content of your presentation is sufficient for them to consider and possibly make a decision regarding the material, so when you ask them are they happy for you to proceed you have completed the first steps to getting to yes! You all know this stuff! Let's look at the slide for an example

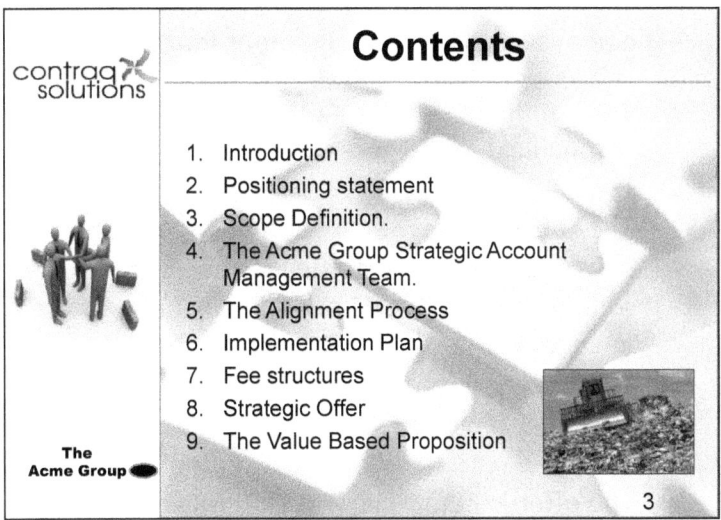

The next slide is your strategic Positioning Statement:

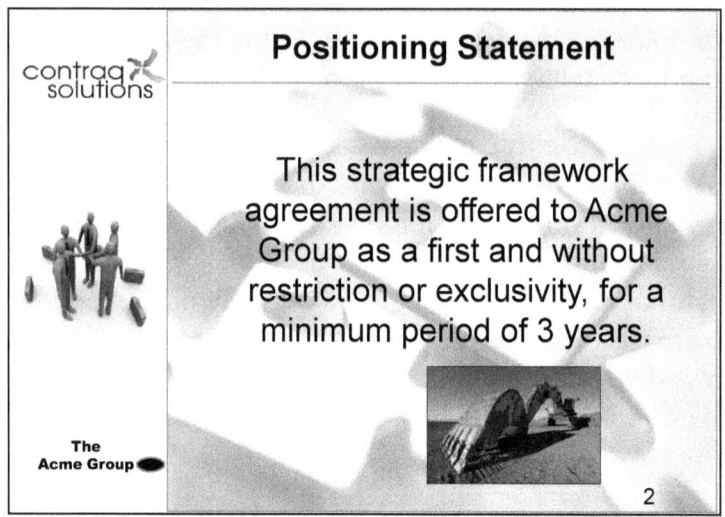

The above slide tells the customer four things:

- The offer is valid for their entire group of companies.

- **The offer is made as a first**. This could be construed by the customer as meaning that this offer is the first of its kind you have offered anyone or the offer is the first in their industry, both scenarios are good and can make the customer feel special.

- The offer is non exclusive! That means it doesn't interfere with any of their current arrangements and poses no threat to their corporate governance.

- The offer is subject to a minimum 3 year contract.

This is a lot of information on one slide with very little detail. Someone told me the other day that if you have more than 30 words on a PowerPoint slide it's no longer a slide it's a word document!

Your next slide should list your scope definition in simple bullet form. You don't have to go into great detail as you can refer to your framework agreement document in front of them. However, you have to capture the main elements of your offered scope as defined in chapter10.

9 Slides to go. What's next?

An organisational chart of your account management team. Remember these org charts from our previous discussions.

All you have to do is explain the roles, functions, reporting lines and responsibilities of all the players depicted on the organogram. The detail is in your framework agreement.

Make these slides as simple as possible! Remember you're building a slide, not an instruction manual! You can put as much detail into the written framework agreement offer as you like. Here we need an illustration of the management team's roles and reporting structure so keep it KISS.

That's the beauty of the org chart; they can say so much, so quickly!

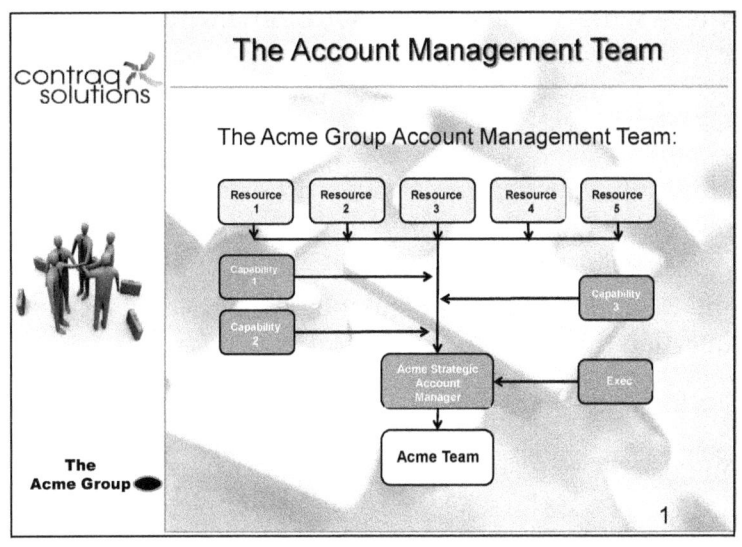

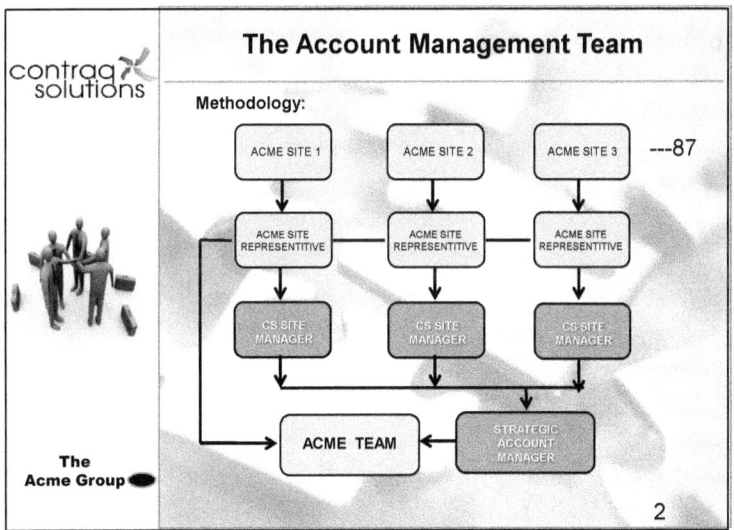

These slides will generate a lot of interaction with the customer which is what you want! (More on this later)

Ok what's next?

The slide depicting the alignment process you propose or you're CRM Plan. All you have to do is show the customer you have a plan for their CRM needs. Just list the topics for discussion and move one. They will rarely question this initially

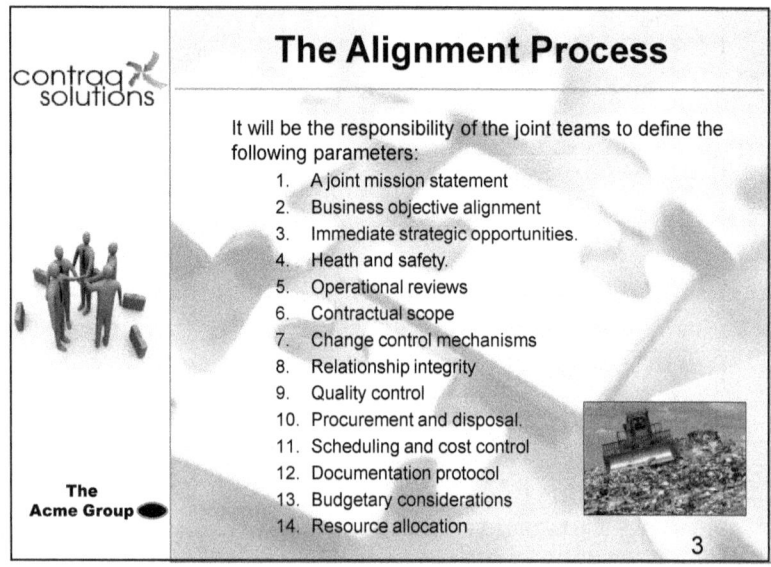

Next you have to build a slide showing your Implementation Plan.

This slide should be in bullet form, indicating the plan in Phases.

While we're on this point, I remember talking to you about not trying to remember your presentation word for word. Well this is where progressive exposure of the information you put on a slide comes in.

Don't put too much information up on a slide all at once. The customer will simply shoot ahead and read it for themselves and the important information you are telling them is lost!

Using bullets is a great way of prompting you, the presenter, on what you need to talk about next. Use a remote mouse, click on the bullet, glance at the screen and you know immediately where you are and what you need to say next! Just fill in the gaps for the customer. This shows you in depth knowledge of the subject and keeps your slides simple and not so busy!

Your next 4 slides are easy; they comprise the following and are excerpts from your framework agreement document!

- A slide detailing the fee structure you are offering the customer (if any?) and your payment terms.

- Your strategic offer detailing all of the incentives you are offering the customer within your proposal (detailed previously)

- Your value based proposition (as detailed previously)

- And finally a summary slide covering all the points you have made within your presentation.

To my reckoning that still leaves you with 1 slide, there you go, more than enough to do the job!

The need for a summary slide will be covered later. However you are going to need one if you intend to close this deal!

That's right, close!

Oh hell! I can hear the groans from here! If you are not a good closer, or you feel awkward closing a deal this is not the game for you, Get out of Dodge now! We will spend some time understanding the psychology of closing later.

Now we need to explore the reason we plan for customer interaction in our presentation.

Interaction

Why do we want interaction with our customer's during our presentation? Well, without it how are we going to know how well we are doing? Customer interaction is an essential part of your presentation plan. However, it would be very dangerous to ask a question, or worse, make a statement to a customer if you were not sure of the way in which they will react! So you have to plan interaction like a strategy. What will you ask to whom and when? What will be the objective?

You should ask the questions you already know the answers to! The questions that arise out of the decision criteria that the customer has informed you you're going to have to cover in your presentation!

If you ask them the question, re-establish its importance in the customer's mind, and then show them your solution to the problem, one by one, you can remove these barriers to entry and establish your credibility and the value of your proposal.

Interaction facilitates customer buy in to the initiatives you are presenting! Discussion and agreement secured from the customer on important points raised in your presentation results in them having to take some level of ownership of these initiatives.

As more and more of these initiatives are discussed and agreed the more vested in the process the customer becomes! This of course is what we want. The ultimate goal is to achieve a position where the customer begins to think all this was their own idea in the first place!

Wow! Why didn't we think of this before?

So that's why we build our presentations with the minimum amount of slides to get over our point, as we want to spend at least half of our allotted time in constructive engagement with the customer!

The next part of your presentation plan is to take advantage of Neuro Linguistic Programming techniques (NLP)

NLP Techniques

In my first book, selling in the 21st century, I spent quite a lot of time explaining the power of using NLP techniques in the selling process. I do not intend in this work to rehash that work here. However, I will explain the basic reasons we have to take NLP into consideration when we build and deliver presentations to our customers.

The first central pre superstition in Neuro Linguistic Programming is that human beings do not all think alike!

Wow, this Guy's a genius! You think!

Well I can imagine what you are thinking right now, but let me explain. Human beings have been proven not to think alike at a Neurological level!

It appears, we choose to make sense of reality around us by processing this data in different parts of our brains to that used by others!

What's more surprising is, if you take a cross section of people from anywhere in the world and test them, the same results appear! You can divide the whole human race into 4 categories of thinkers and the percentages of each are roughly the same everywhere you look!

Visual, audio, kinaesthetic and neutral! These descriptors derive from the fact that we use our five senses we are given, sight, hearing, touch ,smell and taste to process everything that goes on around us!

(All of us except women of course who have many more senses than us men but won't tell us what they are!)

This filtering of reality is called a representational system. And all human beings, it appears, have them, they act like filtering systems on the reality around us 'reality isn't like it is - it's like you are!'

People tend to favour a specific way of thinking and use this process their entire lives. The first centre of their brain they choose to process any data resulting from reality denotes their filtering style or representation system. For example, if you are a Visual filterer you will choose to use the visual centres of your brain before any other neurological ability to process even dialogue! You will create pictures of the conversation someone is having with you! The representational systems can look like this:

Visual		Audio
Audio	or	Visual
Kinaesthetic		Kinaesthetic

These are just 2 examples, the representational system a person favours can be any or all of these combinations. These representational systems are a step process as depicted. In the first one the person thinks first using the visual centres of their brain, then the centres of their brain that processes sound and dialogue and then the kinaesthetic centres of their brain that handles emotion, taste and smell!

Other peoples step process or representational system may be totally different as depicted in the second group. Many combinations are possible. This makes it quite hard to communicate!

If you are dealing with a person who is the same as you, you will get on like a house on fire, however if they are different to you, eh, not so much!

Whatever your representational system is will dictate to a large extent the way you talk and write and to a greater or lesser degree your predictable behaviour given any specific environmental stimulus!

You think like you talk like you write like you act!

This is true with one exception! You may have noticed above that one filtering type is a neutral! These people are very rare, as they represent only 5% of the world's population. These people don't have a representational system, and they think with all of their neurological capabilities at once. They parallel process everything!

These people may come across as very clever. Be careful. NLP has no effect on your IQ. They may sound like leader material and appear exceptionally strong in character but they can be as thick as a brick! (Hitler was one!)

I'm a visual filterer; I use a lot of visual descriptors in my speech patterns and the way I write. I will even say "I see what you mean!" How can you see what someone means? That makes no sense to some people, but it does to me! You may, in the past have had to explain something to someone and they just don't seem to get it? Your explanation is logical and simple, to you!

However, if you are trying to explain road directions to a visual person, after the first intersections forget it! Their eyes start to gloss over and you will hear a lot of ah ha noises but they really need a map dude! They don't think in sound and dialogue - they think in pictures!

The good thing going for you when you build a business presentation is that in research it appears that over 60% of all males on the planet are visual filterers. (Oh, you don't have to tell that to my wife.) That's why, if used correctly, PowerPoint is such a great medium to present in because its multimedia based! The audio's can listen to you and the visuals can look at the pictures!

There is much, much more to NLP than this, but suffice it to say, if you are going to build a presentation to your customers, be aware that the people sitting in the room are made up of a mixture of all these filterers, you have to cater for all of them as much as you can!

Be careful, how you write the slides; try to encompass neutral phrases and not your own filtering traits!

The last important part of all this is simple. If 60% of the people in that room are visual, use as much subliminal material in your slides as possible to build the bridges as I have described earlier. It works real well!

What's next? Oh yes! The subliminal content, that's no coincidence, is it?

Subliminal elements

Having just finished the section on NLP Techniques you must by now appreciate the importance of using subliminal pictures in your presentation to create positive associations in your visual filtered customers!

What will work best?

Well, the customer's own images, ones they are familiar with and represent the culture, branding and corporate citizenship they project!

Where can you get these images? From their websites and company magazines! As mentioned previously, many years ago, to put these customised elements into a presentation, would cost you a fortune. You had to have your material printed professionally, now it's a snip!

Use your cell phone camera to take pictures of your customer's buildings and facilities. (A word of caution here, be circumspect, in today's world, all you would need to do is get arrested by homeland security for taking pictures of strategic sites, so beware!)

Use your phone to capture pictures from their internal magazines and down load images, quotes and logos from their website! This effort won't be lost on them, I assure you!

Use these images in both your framework agreement document and your presentation. Don't go mad! There is such a thing as overkill, but a selection of these images dotted throughout your proposal and presentation will work well!

Next we will explore the oldest trick in the book for getting your message across in advertising and sales, the three tells!

The Three Tells

Tell them what you are going to tell them. Tell them. And tell them what you have just told them!

That's it!

Why? Firstly, because your customer will want a structured introduction to your presentation! They will also have to tune in to your speaking style and you want them to buy in to the content of your presentation.

Secondly if your use the 'third tell' you can use your summary of your material and the highlights of the presentation to launch into your closing augment! (Closing comes next)

The other important part of the three tells approach is that if you can't get agreement from the customer to proceed at the end of your presentation, you leave them with a list of the most important elements of the discussion fresh in their mind. This is the message they leave the room with!

In addition, if any of them have misunderstood anything you have presented by restating your summary of the events you may be able to correct these misunderstandings before they leave the room!

It is for this reason I strongly recommend you start your presentation and end your presentation with a contents and summary slide!

Tell them what you are going to tell them and at the end tell them what you've' told them!

The Close

Why close? If the material is good enough and you've hit all the right buttons the customer will want to buy it right?

No wrong!

I could tell you that the difference between a good sales person and a really great one is their ability to close!

But I won't!

Instead I'll focus on why we should attempt to close the deal at the end of our presentation because of the psychological effect it has on the customer! But first, let me tell you a story!

Many years ago in my prior life I was an executive sales director for a fortune 100 company! I had a lot of sales people reporting to me, many of which thought they could walk on water and a few that could!

All of these professionals had one common fault, they were arrogant! This is par for the course; they wouldn't be as good at their job if they weren't.

It comes with the territory!

My biggest challenge was to get them to understand they must put themselves in a subordinate position to that of the customer and ask nicely for the deal!

My specialised software engineers were the worst. You couldn't leave them alone with a customer for longer than 5 minutes otherwise we would end up picking up the bill for 6 weeks psychiatric counselling for the customer! They had no problem at all in insulting the customer's intelligence and telling them their mother dressed funny!

Seriously I had a big problem! I eventually commissioned a study on why fortune 500 companies award contract to suppliers. What were the overriding factors that convinced the customer that this, or that supplier, was the right choice for the job?

I was astonished with the results! In over 68% of all the respondents in the survey, the main reason given for choosing a supplier in a competitive scenario was the fact the supplier had asked for the order! Go figure!

Price and performance were rated high, of course, but if there was no significant difference in the customers mind the overriding decision maker was the enthusiasm and sincerity of the supplier to want the work!

The customers stated that if the supplier was prepared to ask for the order the customer was of the opinion that the supplier really wanted and needed the work and therefore would be prepared to work with the customer to ensure the success of the venture.

Once I shared this Data with my teams things changed a little, some of them got it and some didn't. However when it came to the incentive schemes and the associated awards that year it was plain to see who had taken this initiative on board and who hadn't!

Then things changed!!

So, there you have it! You have to try and close the deal, ask for the order! Strategise in your team what kind of closing argument you will make, who will do it and to whom will you direct it?

Remember at the end of your presentation, once you have summarised what's been discussed is the perfect time to do it, so build it into your strategy and practice, practice, practice!

The only thing left to discuss in your framework presentation plan is your contingency plan.

The contingency plan

I'm sure I don't have to tell you it's essential to build a contingency plan! But you'll be surprised how many times this is totally overlooked by organisations. Oh, it will be fine, we've done this a thousand times, nothing will go wrong, if, it does we'll handle it!

Yeah right!

I can tell you from my own experience of presenting solutions to customers for 40 years that everything can go wrong! And catastrophically! It's not about luck its Murphy's Law!

When you think you have covered all the bases, wham, he takes your legs out from under you! You cannot ever, be over prepared!

Earlier we talked about checking out your customer's venue if you have to present there. I have attended a presentation recently where my client has not done this, even though I nagged him about it, and pitched up to deliver their organisational changing presentation to find the colour settings on the customers Data projector had either failed or been tampered with!

The result, nearly all of the information within their presentation was eligible! The customer couldn't do anything about it and my Client had brought the presentation on a tinny notebook PC. This resulted in my Client having to walk the customer through their presentation on this small notebook screen, nobody could see and their presentation turned into a disaster. One of the customers called it a Day and said leave the agreement offer with us and we'll get back to you! Oh dear! My Client is still waiting! They have lost all the initiative and momentum they would have had if they had presented as planned.

I once spent three weeks coaching my own sales team on a very important customer presentation only to have myself and the head presenter stuck in the lift on the 3rd floor of the Sheraton Hotel in San Francisco, that's right, you guessed it, it was 1989, the day the 6.8 earthquake hit! (Thank god the big game was on that Day as the Nimitz freeway was almost empty. I often shudder when I think of the consequences if that hadn't been the case!)

The rest of my team made the presentation but no one could deliver the presentation! You would think the customer would have rescheduled this one wouldn't you, given the circumstances, but they said "Everybody else managed to make their presentation so sorry, no, we can't. We don't have the time"

You may think this is really bad luck, but it's not, it was very poor planning on my behalf! I have never forgotten that, I should never have agreed to such a late slot in the day for this presentation in the first place. Ever since that event I insisted on having two presenters to back each other up and I insisted they travelled in different cars!

Let's look at some of the thing you must think of in your contingency plan.

- Always check out the customer's venue and equipment.
- Check the lighting, can you dim the lights?
- Take a large screen laptop.
- Make sure you lap top is fully charge to last at least 1 Hour.
- Take the power cord with you.
- Take your presentation on a flash drive as backup.
- Don't rely on the customers WIFI to down load Data.
- Take extension leads with you.
- Take two pin plugs and adaptors with you.
- Take thick non permanent marker pens with you.
- Take organisational reference material with you.
- Always arrange a caucus room for your team.
- Split your team in different vehicles.
- Train 2 main presenters.
- Be prepared to use the white board or a flip chart to present your proposal.
- Depending where you are in the World prepare for power outages.

- Take as many specialists as you think you may need. Don't have them in the room but handy just in case you need them.

Ok, well that's it, that's your presentation contingency plan!

Let's summarise this chapter:

Chapter Summary:

To prepare for your framework agreement presentation, consider the following strategy plan elements and recommendations:

- **Schedule**
    - Take care to build a comprehensive schedule plan encompassing enough time to build and practice your presentation. Remember you are going to have to do three dry runs!

- **Timing.**
    - Consider the timing aspects of the presentation, the when, what time and duration of the delivery. Always present last, mornings are better than afternoons!

- **Territory.**
    - Consider the territory aspects of your strategy. Always attempt to host the presentation. If they come, they are interested!

- **Room layout**.
    - The room layout is important. U shaped table, data projector, split up

the customers. Use name tags and check out the facility if you have to go to them.

- **The Customers Decision Criteria.**
  - o Ascertain the decision criteria before you present.
  - o Build the criteria into your framework offer strategy.
  - o Engage with the customer on each point.

- **Presentation Team**.
  - o Team dynamics are essential. Plan the Who, the when and how your team will interact. Practice the responses for concerns, objections and obstacles you think may come up.

- **Content.**
  - o Based on 40 minutes presentation time you can only present 12 slides. Build the content around your framework offer strategy with an introduction and summary slide. Keep it KISS!

- **Interaction.**
  - o This is an essential part of your presentation. Build it in to your strategy. What questions will you ask, to whom and strategise the objectives.

- **NLP Techniques.**
  - o Take the possible effects of your customer's NLP filtering into consideration when building and delivering your presentation.

- **Subliminal Elements.**
  - o Take advantage of subliminal images in both your framework agreement document and your presentation. Obtain these images from your customers website

- **The Three Tells.**
  - o Tell them what you are going to tell them, tell them, and tell them what you've told them! Use the third tell to launch your closing argument.

- **The Close.**
  - o Close, close, close! If you don't someone else might!

- **The contingency plan.**
  - o Always have one! If you don't you might come face to face with Murphy when you least expect it!

Well it's done! That's your framework agreement strategy finished! **But have we finished yet?**

If the customer likes your framework agreement they may want to negotiate with you (remember I mentioned your position of strength earlier) well to complete these selling strategies let's take a look at a negotiation strategy plan to complete your Combat Zone arsenal, it's the last initiative we cover in this work.

20.

The Negotiation Strategy Plan

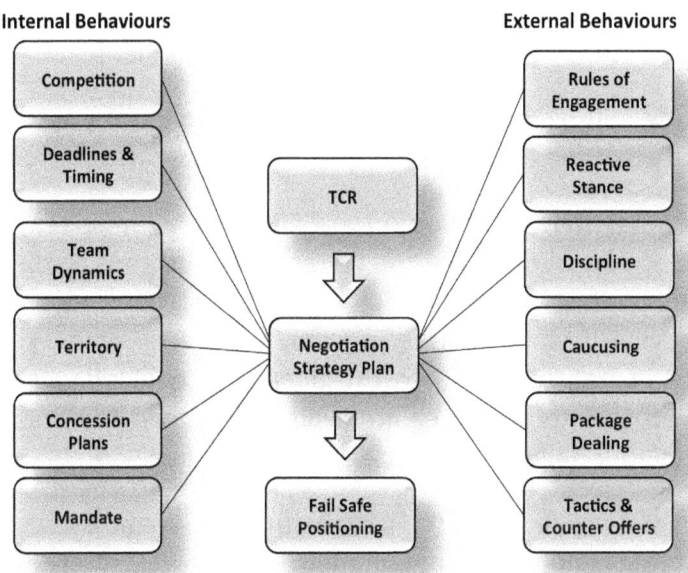

I have written extensively on the subject of negotiation in my previous books, so I do not intend to go into too much detail here other than to go through the above plan to highlight some of the more important strategies you must not overlook when preparing to negotiate with your customer.

The Technical Client Review (TCR)

The importance of a TCR cannot be understated as it can change the expectations and mind set of the customer before they receive your presentation or proposal! The Guerrilla Warfare tactic is to sell up and sell forward at the TCR to out manoeuvre your competition.

They will bid to the original specification and you can bid all of the added extras and alternatives in addition!

In a negotiation scenario the TCR provides sales teams an opportunity to test the water when it comes to their selling strategy and price! At a TCR you can identify specific threats or risks you may encounter when you are invited to negotiate the deal! This enables you to build countermeasures into your bid before you quote and your negotiation strategy to nullify these risks!

Always try to conduct TCR's before you commit to any strategy, pricing or negotiation process. It can change your chances of winning the Deal!

Competition

As in your account pursuit strategy plan we must always consider our position of strength as compared to any competitor when entering into negotiation with the customer. In the case of your framework agreement offer you will be in competition with the customers current supplier, however as we have said previously you have a major advantage in this scenario as your competitor has no idea what you have proposed and has to play catch-up!

But be aware! That does not mean they are not capable of matching your offer! In any situation in sales you have to seriously consider the competitive scenario when building your concession plan to win the deal (more on this a little later)

Go through the same process as in the account pursuit strategy plan it will give you an insight into your competitors strengths and weaknesses.

When conducting the TCR a good question to ask the customer is "with your current service provider, if you could change any parameter of their service to you, what would that be?" This question is investigative and non- threatening, it generally results in the customer telling you some interesting facts regarding the current relationship with their current supplier! There will always be something they would like to change, pricing, and delivery performance is a common response. You can use this information to your advantage when called to negotiate the deal!

Deadlines and Timing

In negotiation as in presenting there is a right time and a wrong time to negotiate. Review the chapter on timing in our presentation strategy. The most important thing to remember when negotiating is not to let the customer stall you until your deadlines are reached! This is a favourite trick of the supply chain. Don't run out of time!

In regards to timing, like presenting to win, always negotiate last! (We will cover the rules of engagement just now)

Always try to establish your customer's deadline. This gives you the edge, don't be in a hurry to meet with them, the more time you give them after the negotiation, the more time they have to find alternatives and build strategy against you for the next round!

Knowing your customer's deadline for delivery or completion of any venture or project is an extremely important piece of information!

In your negotiation strategy always try to build in some accelerated performance on delivery as an ace in the whole! If you can provide them with an additional week of production, the profit this generates for the customer gives your team a massive position of strength.

The money this represents generally makes your competitive pricing position irrelevant as you have now reframed the negotiation into the performance arena not the price and your competitor has not!

This is especially important if the customer is negotiating with you last!

Team Dynamics

As in presentation, try very hard to never negotiate alone! This is suicide against the modern Day supply chain team; they will cut you to pieces before you can say Donald Trump! You need to be well represented, with one team leader; the head negotiator, to lead the team and field all questions and answers unless they need the team to support them.

Never jump into a negotiation without being asked by your team leader to participate. You may end up volunteering strategic information to your opponent!

Talking is the single biggest problem I encounter in negotiation. Sales teams tend to think a negotiation is a debate situation! Sometimes, even a selling opportunity!

Bye the time you have reached the customer's negotiating table the time for debate is over!

Now is the time to shut up and listen to what the customer wants!

You will either be able to provide them with what they want or you won't. If you are in a strong position stop selling and start negotiating. If you have built strong positioning you will be able to negotiate alternatives and options to satisfy the customer's needs

There a lot more details in the negotiation strategy plan document regarding communication techniques amongst team members but as I have said previously if you want one just drop me a mail.

Territory

Again, it is important to attempt to host the customer negotiations on your own home turf! If the customer accepts your invitation what does it tell you about your positioning?

Be aware, in this scenario the customer can always use limited authority or lack of information when they come to you, so make sure if they come, they have full mandate to negotiate!

Concession plans

The most important part of your negotiation strategy plan will be to set your concession plans! You need to consider your Zones of potential agreement (ZOPA) and your best alternatives to a negotiated agreement (BATNA) on everything you think you may well have to negotiate!

What will you have to give to get what you want? What is your platinum, gold and brass deals on any parameter you may be asked to negotiate?

Setting your hearts on the best deal for you would be the worst thing you can do!

Shoot for it, but consider, what would be the worst possible deal you would accept, to secure the contract!

Create visual representations of your maximum and minimum wins in exchange for your maximum and minimum concessions you will offer in return. Do not make the ranges (ZOPA) between best and worse very big as you may find you are giving away more than you have to in a fair and reasonable exchange.

For more details on this process see Combat Zone. "Negotiating in the new Millennium'

The graphic below is an example from the negotiation strategy plan to help you build your concessions.

Building Fail Safe Concessions Plans

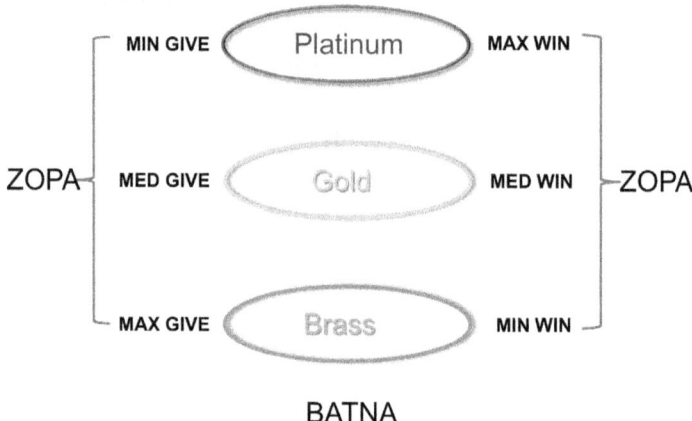

BATNA

In the above graphic the gives are your concessions (what you are prepared to offer the customer). The wins are things you want from the customer in return for those concessions.

The Platinum ring is your best objective the brass ring the worst. The gold ring is your fall back condition in case you can't secure your platinum deal.

Giving yourselves three strategic positions between best situation and worst situation allows you two levels of failsafe positioning. Any deal you can arrive at between the identified zones of potential agreement is fine.

Mandate

It is important to negotiate with mandate. That's why we build concession plans so our executive can fully appreciate what we think it might take to secure a contract.

To negotiate from a position of strength we have to have concessions and a walk away price sanctioned by senior management.   This gives you confidence to negotiate from a position of strength!

The rules of engagement

- **Less is more!**

Do not volunteer strategic information or concessions unless you really have to!

- **Always negotiate last!**

You will never be able to shake hands if you go first! (We have covered this previously)

- **Always negotiate as close to your opponent's deadline as possible.**

This limits flexibility and introduces an element of pressure to reach agreement!

Reactive stance

Never be proactive in a negotiation! Let your customer play out their hand before you react with any concessions. Insist they table all of their requirements before you consider the deal on the table.

Here is a negotiation style that is safe, simply follow the sequence of events!

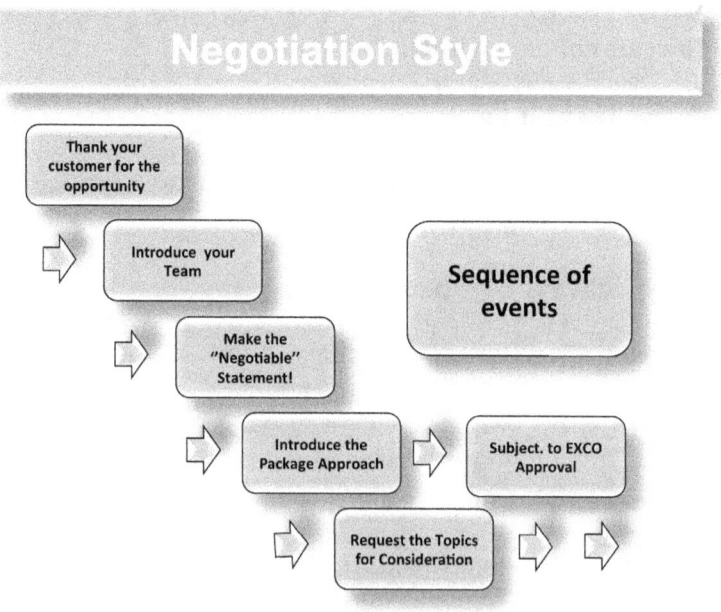

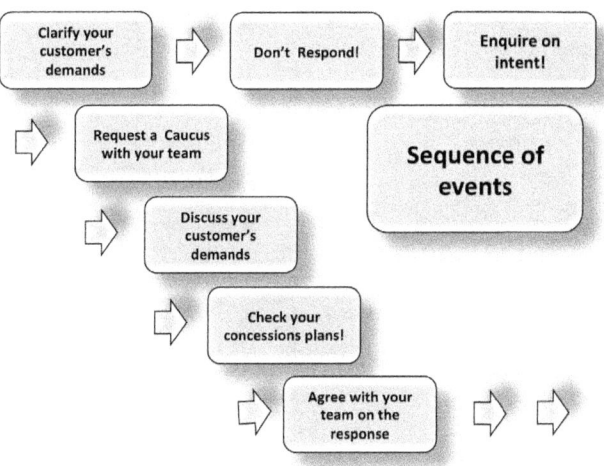

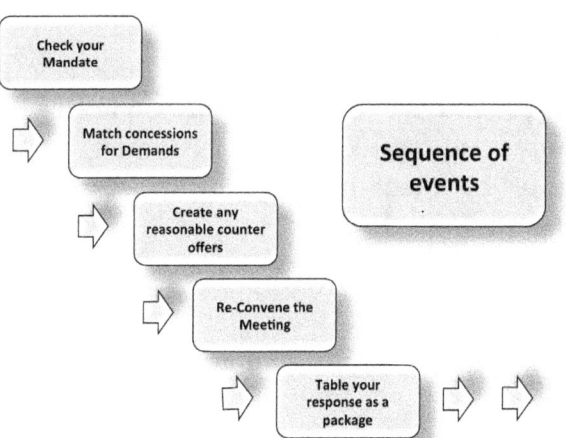

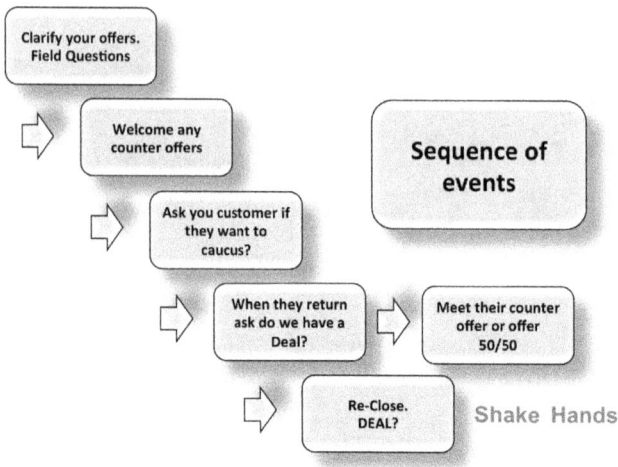

Clarify your offers. Field Questions

Welcome any counter offers

Ask you customer if they want to caucus?

When they return ask do we have a Deal?

Meet their counter offer or offer 50/50

Re-Close. DEAL?

Sequence of events

Shake Hands

Let's explain the sequence:

As soon as you sit down at the table take the opportunity to thank your customer for the opportunity to meet with them to discuss your proposal.

Let them know you are very keen to work with them to reach agreement and win this deal.

Take the opportunity to introduce your team

Identify their roles in the negotiation (why are they there) however, explain your position as lead negotiator and that you will address any questions the customer may have.

Introduce the negotiable statement!

That is that you are happy to negotiate any parameter of your proposal with the customer on the condition that it leads to your organisation being awarded the contract (that sets the scene, you are there to negotiate for the contract, cut to the chase!)

The next goal would be to introduce the package deal approach.

Advise the customer you and your team would prefer it if the customer, would table all of their questions and requirements as a package for your team's consideration.

If you get any resistance from the customer, simply state you team will have to view all of the parameters holistically, as all the elements are inextricably linked to performance and price. (That will confuse them!)

Another important step (unless you are an executive director of your company) is to advise the customer that all discussions can be agreed to in principle but will ultimately will be subject to your executive board's approval!

This is your get out of jail card! You are negotiating for and on behalf of your shareholders but you are not legally responsible for any outcome. You need to indemnify yourself and your team!

Step six is to request the customer's questions and make notes.

Ask as many questions as necessary to understand their needs but do not under any circumstances address any of these individual topics until you understand the entire list!

Clarify the customer's requirements

Make sure your team fully understands what the customer wants, ask them if they would like to ask the customer any specific questions but don't let them respond.

Introduce the customer commitment question

Once you are satisfied that you and your team fully understand the customer's needs you can ask a very important question in regard to the customer's intent!

"So, if we are able to address all of these topics to you team's satisfaction, are you in a position to award us the contract?"

Watch their reaction carefully, it will tell you if they have any additional items that they are holding back, this is a tactic called escalation and is designed to ambush you at the very end of a negotiation.

You statement generally results in them telling you the whole story before you caucus with your team.

Ask the customer for a caucus

Discuss their requirement with your team in private!

You can tell them you need to contact head office for some support for your decisions. Say anything you want, just get out of Dodge to discuss the topic in private.

Discuss all of the customer's requests in detail!

Make sure your team fully understands the ramifications of all of the topics tabled by the customer.

Check your concession plans for ZOPA

Look for any relationships between money, performance, down payments and or offered deposits in any of the topics the customer has raised, these relationships can be the answer to making this deal!

Check your mandate

Agree on these parameters. And formulate any BATNA offers if the customer's requests are outside of any of your ZOPA.

Fully agree with your team

Agree on the strategy going forward and script your response for all the topic's raised. In short create your packaged deal response. Always leave any savings or discounts to the very end of your packaged offer; they will have greater effect if you do!

Reconvene the meeting with the customer.

Table all of your responses

Table your responses in the form of a package deal. Make sure the customer understands that they cannot unbundle your deal. It's a package deal. **If you do this, this and that, we will give you this, this and this!**

Make the counter offer statement

At this point you can make another very important statement!

"If you feel strongly enough about any element of our package deal we are open to any counter offers you would like to make, as long as if, we agree to them, you award us the contract!"

This may result in them responding with a counter offer, but it will be contingent on them awarding you the contract! **Bah Boom!**

Let the customer caucus

They may want to discuss your offer in private so let them.

If they come back with a counter offer you cannot afford, tell them and make an offer to split the additional demand 50/50, or split the difference as they generally ask for more than they need! This tactic is generally sufficient to reach agreement.

ASK DO WE HAVE A DEAL

Shake hands!

Discipline

Your negotiation team needs to have discipline. The team leader fields all questions and answers from the customer unless they feel they need your help! Do not be tempted to jump in and help them, you will probably give strategic positioning away. You don't know what your team leader has in mind. However if they are sinking the ship, that's different. Interrupt them and call for a caucus to discuss the matter. Be diplomatic! Your negotiation team needs to be like the formula 1 pit crew. Everyone knows their job, right!

Caucusing

Once you have all of your customer's requirements on the table, don't be tempted to launch into your package deal immediately the customer needs to believe their demands have merit and need consultation. If you jump to a solution to quickly they may think they have been too lenient on you! Caucus with your team and take half an Hour to discuss it in private!

Package dealing

Never allow your opponent to piece meal you in negotiation. What I mean is do not respond to the agenda items one at a time. This is extremely dangerous, you are committing to something before you know what the next agenda item is or means! Always insist your customer places all of their topics for discussion on the table before you commit to anything! Turn the negotiation into a package deal!

Tactics and countermeasures

Make sure you and your team are familiar with all of the common tactics and strategies, along with their countermeasures before you negotiate. I will not go into detail here as most of you know this game well. However, if you don't, talk to me or look them up on the internet.

- The 50/50 split.
- Splitting the difference.
- The nibble.
- Escalation. Good or bad.
- Non-negotiable demands.
- Emotional outbursts.
- Good cop, bad cop.
- Cheery picking.
- Limited authority.
- Leveraging upfront payments and deposits.
- Deferring Issues.
- Scope creep.
- Off the record discussions.
- Changing negotiators.
- Continuous caucusing.
- Shared responsibility.
- Party negotiations.
- Stalling

Ok, now we are finished!

With the negotiation strategy plan complete your Combat Zone arsenal is complete!

All we need to do now is summarise and close

21.

Summary

At the beginning of this book we talked about the challenge of capturing new business, while keeping care of the business we have, and to do this while the world is going through one of the worst recessions in history! It's tough out there and that's for sure, but you know the adage when the going gets tough the tough get? No, not drinking!

Business has to go on, but, if there's not a lot of business about, that's also Ok as long as you are getting the lions share! But that's not going to happen if you are playing the same game and playing by the same rules as your competitors! To win you are going to have to change both!

In this work I have shared six initiatives with you:

The value based proposition

Focusing your customer's attention on the value based proposition rather than the price of your products or service.

This initiative seems to have been forgotten by all but the initiated few. Forget trying to compete on price, you're playing directly into the hands of your customer's supply chain and your competitors. Focus your customer's attention on the time it takes your product to pay for itself, and starts making money for them! Your price, compared to their production profit is a fraction, don't forget it!

The benchmark survey approach

Opening new customer doors by using a market specific benchmarking survey approach. Who wouldn't want to participate in a benchmarking survey specifically aimed at your industry and get to see the results! This is a great way to open doors and a lot of them at once! This strategy can fill up your sales pipeline with real opportunities overnight.

What sales organisation wouldn't want to try it, especially as it only takes one survey customer visit per week by each of your sales people to pull off!

Account pursuit plans.

Using account pursuit plans to build strategy as a team before approaching a customer with any value based proposition.

Five days planning is worth three months hard work! Using account pursuit plans enables more people in the organisation to participate in the strategy planning phase of any customer pursuit. It minimises errors in judgement on the sales team part early in the pursuit process and introduces the concept and culture of the organisational calibration for success! Account pursuit plans help sale teams develop discipline and a more comprehensive value based proposition approach to sales opportunities.

A customer relationship management plan (CRM)

A CRM plan! To help you manage your existing customers. CRM assists in the challenge of turning your strategic customer into a revenue and profit centre for your organisation, selling up and selling forward becomes easier and building the relationship based on agreed to working methodology creates value for both. CRM increases the barriers of entry for any competitor!

However, beware, this role is not normally undertaken by your sales people! You need a special animal for this role, the strategic account manager (SAM)

Remember CRM can act as the glue between the two!

A Framework Agreement strategy Plan

An unsolicited framework agreement can upset the positioning of the entrenched competitor and open doors to new business! In any field of operation, it's the guerrilla warfare sales tactic. More importantly, it appears to be one of the game changing strategies that is currently being used to capture business to business business (BBB) internationally. It could possibly represent the singular most significant initiative your organisation could adopt to change the current competitive status quo in your business!

A negotiation strategy plan

If your customer likes your framework agreement you may well find yourself sitting at the negotiation table. Build your concessions plans carefully and don't forget your ZOPA and BATNA positions.

I believe that all sales teams need these six strategy initiatives and in- house strategy documents, as part of their modern Combat Zone Arsenal!

Business is very hard to come by these days so my advice is to really focus on your target customers, don't allow you sales team to shotgun sell! Calibrate your organisation for success by creating value based propositions in your pursuit plans and transpose them into open framework agreement proposals to gain entry or cement the relationship you have with these valuable customers.

Remember if you need any copies of these in house strategy templates; just mail us, I would be happy to help!

In addition for a small financial consideration and an Air Ticket, I will come and help you build your own, and secure your first BBB framework agreement!

I won't wish you good luck as sales people make their own, so go! Capture some new business and until next time, Cheers!